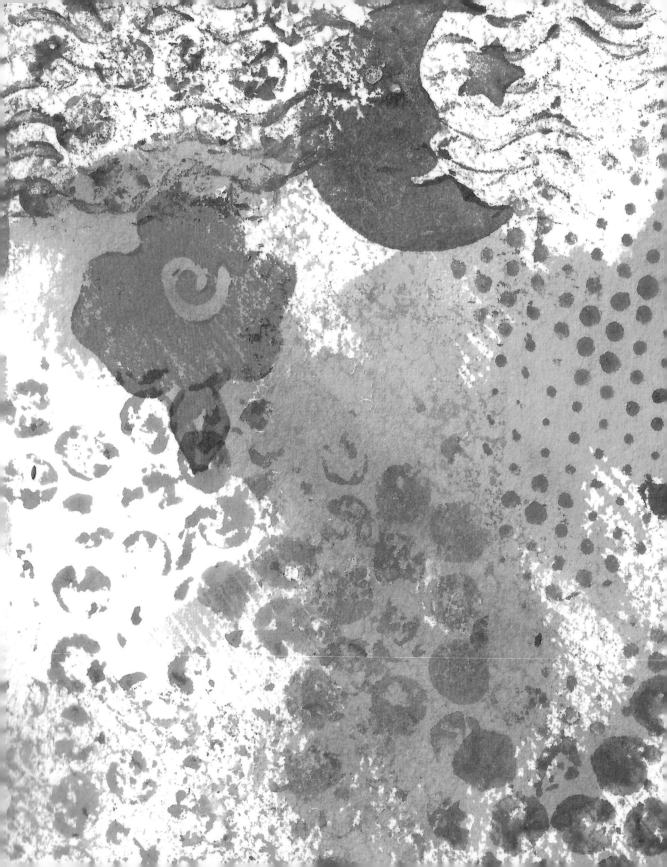

Dear Jacqui,
Here's to an organized &
colorful life!   xo,

Nicole

THE ART OF
ORGANIZING

eight years

great deal of pain. Dep

uble. It is probably an exagger
capital of one Nordic coun
ed for dru ... en behavior
street.

happiness in you, first
here. But don't say I'm
nothing to do with who
ss in new. The investigate
may have something to do w

95

actions are comm
ad a smiling ex
re is denial, som times
h unhappiness.
the ego play
in other coun
almost the n
The hippie move
ss, and joy ... part of that role
ry seriously. Spontaneity
n you play that

display

THE ART OF ORGANIZING

AN ARTFUL GUIDE TO AN ORGANIZED LIFE

Written by

NICOLE GABAI

Illustrations and artwork
by Nicole Gabai

If you have a chronic problem getting organized, there is help.
Visit www.clutterersanonymous.org for more information.

ISBN: 978-1-7372143-0-4 (Hardcover)

Printed in China

Original Illustrations by Nicole Gabai.
Digitized Illustrations by Farida Zaman.
Artwork by Nicole Gabai.

Design by Weller Smith Design, LLC.

10 9 8 7 6 5 4 3 2 1

First Edition

Published by Nicole Gabai, B. Organized!
www.b-organized.net

Dedication

This book is dedicated to all my B. Organized clients who welcomed me into their homes and offices. You inspired me to write this book.

Table of

CONTENTS

Front of Book

Chapter One

Chapter Two

Chapter Three

"For every minute spent organizing, an hour is earned." —BENJAMIN FRANKLIN

Chapter Four

Chapter Five

Chapter Six

Back of Book

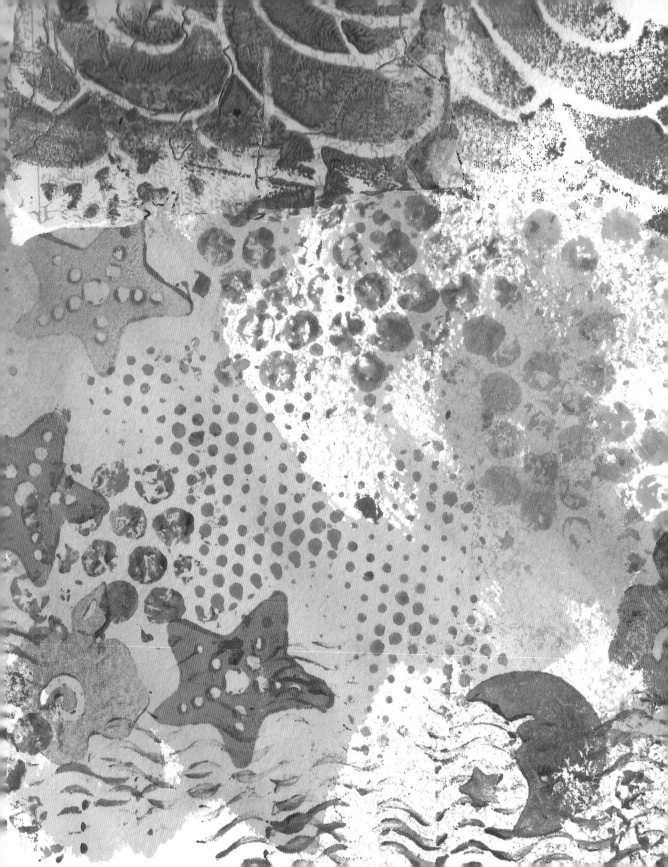

Buenos días, bonjour, and good morning! That's how I started each day when I was a kid. Thanks to Maria, our Peruvian nanny, my French-Peruvian dad, and my American mom, by the time I was seven years old, I was fluent in all three languages.

• • •

possible in life and believed you were never too young to start. It was a whirlwind life and organization became a refuge for me amid the chaos.

I can still vividly remember my kindergarten classroom in Paris. It was set up in neat sections: one section held painting supplies like smocks,

I was born in Lima, Peru, and lived there until I was six years old when we moved to Paris. My parents were adventurous, cultured, and somewhat eccentric, and we traveled a lot during my childhood. They wanted to expose my sister and me to as many experiences as

paints, brushes, and easels; in another section, toys were neatly stored in large cubbies against the wall. There were designated places for toys made of wood, books, pull toys, and little toy animals. It was such a calm environment, and knowing where everything belonged gave a sense of order to my world.

As the new girl in the class, I was shy, and because I was used to speaking some French but mostly Spanish at home, the language differences made me feel a little left out. As I looked around the room filled with kids I didn't know, one toy, in particular, caught my eye. It was a foot-long wooden block with a series of five different-sized brass cylinders that nested neatly into their designated holes. I remember being fascinated and endlessly entertained by this block with its neatly fitting brass cylinders. I found it so

calming to place the cylinders right where they belonged—it was like a puzzle, where each piece gently fit where it needed to be.

At home, there was a lot of chaos. My parents were **bon vivants** and possessed such *joie de vivre*. They enjoyed many late nights out dancing, dining, drinking wine, and socializing into the wee hours. The calm in the storm was Maria, our beloved nanny, friend, and go-to person. She was incredibly organized, neat, tidy, responsible, and loving. She made sure all our linens and clothing were kept beautifully folded in neat little piles in the closets. Even our little-girl underwear was perfectly folded and stacked. Wherever we traveled, from Peru to France to Miami, Florida, where we moved when I was seven, Maria made me feel safe, secure, and very loved.

One day, when I was eight years old, Maria left. At the time, I didn't know why, but I was devastated. (Many years later, we got back in touch, and I learned that she

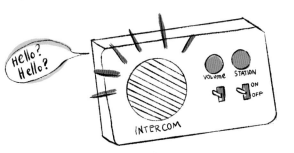

to make projects run more smoothly. After stints working for Nickelodeon, the Orlando Film Commission, and a commercial film production company, I became an actress and model in my early thirties. At the same time, I launched and began developing my organizing business.

had found a better-paying job to support her children back in Peru.) Alone in a new country, one of the things that brought me comfort and made me happy during this time was playing office. While other girls were playing Barbies or dress-up, I would invite some of the girls in our neighborhood to come over and play. We used the intercoms in the bedrooms, prepared envelopes to mail, and played with a stapler, paper clips, old checks, and a rubber stamper.

Little by little, I was developing my organizing gene. When I was sixteen, I left my parents' chaotic home in search of calmer waters and moved in with an aunt who lived nearby. At eighteen, I moved to New York City to go to college. I loved the city's well-organized grid system, which made the streets so easy to navigate. I started my art education at Parsons School of Design, completed my studies and earned a BFA from the Fashion Institute of Technology, and then moved into the world of TV production with a job at MTV. There, I learned the concept of "controlled chaos" and created many systems

—

We used the intercoms in the bedrooms, prepared envelopes to mail, and played with a stapler, paper clips, old checks, and a rubber stamper.

—

I think organizing comes more naturally to some of us than to others. But, with a little practice, it is a skill anyone can learn. For nearly two decades, I have helped hundreds of clients create order out of chaos in their

offices, closets, kitchens, and everywhere in between. In this book, I share with you the secrets that I pass on to all my clients—and the joys of being an artist and creative thinker in an organized world.

Sometimes people think of creativity and organization in opposition to one another. The truth is a good organizational system makes so much more room for creativity. Keeping things organized has given me the freedom to explore my creativity in many ways, including the mixed media art and illustrations you will find throughout the book. I wanted this book to have a whimsical feel to remind you that organizing can be fun!

I encourage you to find the fun in your own organizing projects. Splurge on the colorful file boxes, buy the datebook in a pattern that makes you happy, showcase the pencil cup that reminds you of a mermaid's tail. When you love your organizing tools, it's much easier to stay organized. Make the process delightful—if it doesn't delight you, it probably won't work.

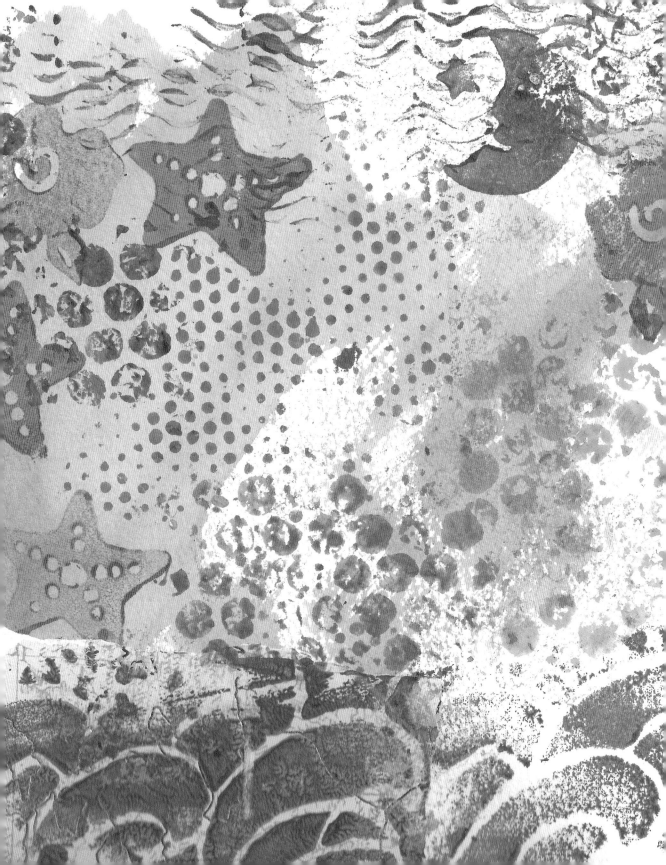

n teacher an
leman
ne provin
red that th
day. he ca
was not yet
m that he

W1

95

ry serious. spontaneity,
t part of that role
the West Co
d through

The hippie moven

ess, and joy

almost the n

in other coun
the ego play
unhappiness.
e is denial, sometime
d a smiling exc
ctions are comm

roles and conception iden

e a true teacher.
d the sameness of bearing
r b gar or king

able. It is probably an exagger
capital of one Nordic coun
rested for dru en behavior
treet.

happiness in you first

there. But don't sa

nothing to do with yo

i no. Then

have something to

eight

ple plays, and

l of pain. Dep

THE SIX ORGANIZING PRINCIPLES

"It takes as much energy to wish as it does to plan."

—ELEANOR ROOSEVELT

When I studied at Parsons School of Design, one of the first things I learned was the importance of the color wheel. As an artist, I use it all the time. When I began writing down my ideas for this book, it occurred to me that this same tool I have used for years in my art corresponded perfectly with the basic six-step process I use to help my clients get organized.

HOLISTIC APPROACH

I believe in a holistic approach to getting organized, meaning that every room in the house is interconnected and each area's organization directly relates to how we manage our time and space. Like the three primary colors on the color wheel, my organizing process has three primary principles that form the foundation for every organizational project. There are also three secondary principles, like the three secondary colors on the color wheel, that will help you put your organizational plan into practice.

The **three primary principles** that we will discuss in Chapters One, Two, and Three are all about how you choose to organize your space: first, by dividing it into **sections**, then by prioritizing your **organizational zones**, and, finally, by choosing the right **storage solutions**.

The second half of this book covers the **three secondary principles** of organizing: **information management**, which will help you take control of all your information and data; **portability**, which will allow you to take your new systems with you on the go; and getting **back to one**, which is essential to maintaining your beautiful new systems.

When all these principles are pulled together, you'll have everything you need to achieve the simplified, streamlined life you want, perfectly customized for you. Being organized brings serenity, happiness, and success wherever you go. It is the foundation upon which a creative and inspired life can truly flourish.

GETTING STARTED

Before we begin working through the six principles in detail, there are a few questions you should ask yourself. Get out a pen and paper, open your laptop, or open the notes app on your phone and answer in as much detail as possible. These following questions are more important than they might appear:

- ⊘ **Why do you want to get organized and why now?**

- ⊘ **What is working for you in your space currently?**

- ⊘ **What is not working in your space as it is now?**

- ⊘ **Which room do you want to begin with?**

- ⊘ **What space causes you the most tension and anxiety or is the most troublesome?**

The answers to these questions will guide you and direct your plan of action, so take the time now to really think about them. I always start by asking my clients what is working in their space, because the right tools for organizing your life are the tools that work best for you. Some people say, "I love drawers," or "I like notebooks," or "I like clear folders." Whatever organizational tools you like best should be incorporated into your plan.

What's not working in your space? If a client says, "I don't like my chair," that's significant. So are a broken lamp, a desk that doesn't feel good, and drawers that stick. These are problems, and they are important pieces of information. If you don't like something, finding a solution you love will make you more likely to use and maintain your new system.

If you have a room you want to begin with, start there, and try to finish organizing that room before you move on to the next. I see the home as an integrated whole, and every room affects every other room, but you can't deal with everything at once. If you try to tackle the whole home at the same time, it's easy to get overwhelmed, so I recommend organizing one room at a time.

If you don't have a specific room you want to begin with, try to identify the most difficult area—the space that is the biggest mess or feels like the biggest challenge. I often ask my clients, "Where is the messiest spot in your house?" or "What space causes you anxiety?"

This is usually where the bottleneck is, and it is often a key to mastering order in the entire home. Once you clear the bottleneck you gain perspective. Dealing with the most challenging spot first is like releasing a relief valve, which then allows the rest of your organizing to fall into place. Your bottleneck might be your kitchen table, your entryway, or the sofa. Since beginning here is the most challenging, you need to stay motivated. Pace yourself and remind yourself why you wanted to get organized in the first place.

The "why" is important, because it is what will keep you motivated. There are many reasons to get organized. Some of the most common I hear are:

"I want to be able to have people over to the house."

"I can't keep living like this."

"My bills are late because I can't find them."

"I want to feel more at peace and not surrounded by clutter."

Whatever your reason, keep it in mind as you begin this journey and use it to motivate you as you continue through the six steps. I've found that getting organized clears your mind so you can get on to the more important things in your life and spend more time doing what you really want to do. When you are organized, you can stop living life reactively, driven by each little crisis, and instead take a more proactive, intentional approach to directing your own life.

the summer. S...d a ...nd over several thousand ...
...rs are in the dai...... business. Pocatello cheese...
...to nearly cheese se... factories. ...well known...... distant markets. ...n the state. ...there are flour mills, beet ...
...sugar... factories, and... frozen-food plants. ...

...nly of who the other...
...especially in relation to...
...o you think you are not relat... ...u think you are related...
...her person is, and vice versa. ...
...has made of yourself, is ...
...he conceptual image ...
...r person's mind ...
...tion be- ...
...four

...n identification with ...
...cause the insanity of the ...
...e hippie movement repre- ...
...tr...lig... ego structures in ...
...e move...e...degen... ...
...ft behin... ...ng ...
...movement...h...made ...
...on...d...inity to

Chapter One

SECTIONAL ORGANIZING

"The best way to get something done is to begin."

—AUTHOR UNKNOWN

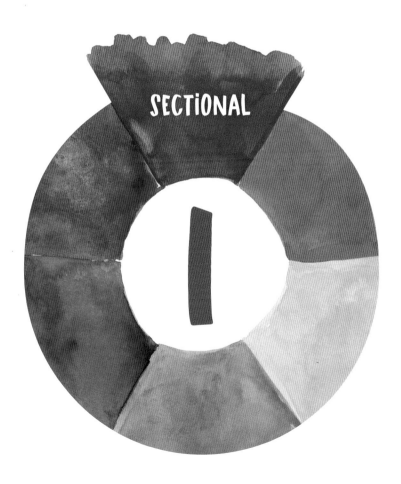

SECTIONAL

1

THE FiRST STEP iN MY ART OF ORGANiZiNG SYSTEM—
THE PRiMARY COLOR RED ON OUR COLOR WHEEL—iS

SECTiONAL
ORGANiZiNG

No matter what type of space you're in, dividing it into sections will set you on the right path to successful organization.

IN SECTIONAL ORGANIZING, each room is divided into areas that correspond to a given activity. To begin, think about what activities you'd like to do in this space. Once you've listed them all, you'll divide the space into corresponding sections and label them. This makes it easy to collect the items that belong in each section so like items are together.

>> **mini TIP:** Always use blue painter's tape when taping your walls. Regular tape will peel your paint.

CHOOSING SECTIONS

For example, let's consider a home office. First, survey the room and think about how your space is currently used, as well as any other activities you might like to do there. Perhaps, in addition to a functional and attractive desk, you need a comfy reading chair. You might also need a place to store your favorite reference books, a cabinet for your creative projects or crossword puzzles, or a place to store your office supplies.

Get some unlined pieces of 8½-x-11-inch paper and write down each activity you plan to do in that room, writing one activity on each page. Then, tape these signs on the walls in the parts of the room you want to designate for each activity. (Use blue painter's tape for this so you don't peel the paint off your walls when you remove the signs.) You'll use the signs as a guide as you begin to sort your belongings into sections.

SUPPLIES CHECKLIST
What You Need for Sectional Organizing

- ⊘ STICKY NOTES
- ⊘ TRASH BAGS
- ⊘ 8½-X-11-INCH SHEETS OF UNLINED PAPER
- ⊘ A BLACK MARKER
- ⊘ BLUE PAINTER'S TAPE
- ⊘ A FEW EMPTY BOXES FOR TEMPORARY HOMES WHILE SORTING
- ⊘ A BOTTLE OF WATER AND A SNACK OR TWO
- ⊘ ONE TO TWO HOURS PER ROOM FOR THE INITIAL SORT

>> **mini TIP:** Plan to spend up to three hours at a time working on your organizing project. Take breaks between each of your three-hour blocks of time. When you are in the depths of sorting, it can be tedious and overwhelming, but if you schedule a break to have a snack, take a walk, hydrate, and step away for a couple of hours, you will return feeling refreshed with the process of adjusting your space before the overwhelm discourages you.

• • •

I recently worked through this process with a client, named Holly, to determine the sections in her home office.

Holly lives with her husband and her 10-year-old daughter in a three-bedroom house. One of the bedrooms is used as her home office, which she shares with her husband. They run a home-based business managing the logistics of selling off-site inventory. Holly felt overwhelmed in their office, which was piled high with papers, stacks of folders, bins of documents, and all kinds of other items scattered everywhere. She mostly knew where things were, but it often took her a while to find what she needed in the disarray. She didn't like the space and didn't feel as though she could relax and focus the way she wanted to.

In addition to tending to her business, Holly styled her daughter's hair every morning in this room and used the space to wrap gifts and store her art supplies. Her office was accommodating a lot of activity, but none of it had a designated place or section.

First, we needed to sort what was in her room and break down the activities Holly used her office for into specifics, then get into the minutiae. It's important to get super specific about everything on, in, and around your desk at least once at the beginning of the organizing process; but the good news is, if you do a thorough job once, you won't really need to go that deep again.

We listed every activity Holly did in her office. I took several unlined 8½-x-11-inch sheets of paper and wrote on each one with a black marker: "art supplies," "hair products," "desk/office products," "gift wrap area," and so on. Then we taped each paper on the wall and began sorting all the items in the room, placing them near the sign for

Kids' Tip:

Young kids often like to be near their parents or near the action. Have a homework area for kids somewhere near whatever you're doing in the afternoon or evening, most likely in the kitchen or living room.

whichever activity they were associated with. You don't have to put the sheet of paper exactly where you'll be doing that activity; it's just a placeholder for the initial sort. The important thing is to allow enough space to physically corral all the items in each section. When you're done sorting the items in the room you're organizing, I suggest going through the rest of the home and gathering up any misplaced items that fit into one of the sections in that room.

Once we had Holly's items sorted into sections, it was easier to logically (or intuitively) determine where in the room was the best place for each activity.

For example, we gathered all hair styling products in a large basket and placed it near her desk in front of a small mirror. The basket was portable, which was handy for the few mornings she might like to style her daughter's hair in the bathroom, but now it had a designated place in the office for most mornings.

When we finished her office, Holly said, *"Oh, I wish I could get my dining room table to look like this!"* Holly's dining room table was her real organizational bottleneck. Holly's family congregated in the kitchen, so the dining room table was piled high with papers, schoolbooks, clothing, and backpacks. The table was the first thing Holly saw when she entered the house and the last thing she saw when she left, and it always bothered her. Here again, we did an initial sort. We put the papers into broad categories and separated newspapers and magazines into one pile.

Then, using sticky notes on file folders, we labeled "papers and flats," "bills," and things related to her "daughter's school." We created a bill-paying section, a regular in-and-out section to ease the flow of bills, and a section to store reading materials so when a particular newspaper or magazine was needed, everyone knew where it was.

Once the office and dining room table were organized, everything else started to fall into place. Holly had a lot more energy and felt reinvigorated enough to tackle her projects. She was inspired to keep going and organize the rest of her home. As she managed her space and time with more ease, she felt there was more room for creativity in her life. She also felt a sense of empowerment and mastery over her stuff. Things that had been buried, hidden, or tossed aside for so long could now be unearthed and handled.

For Holly, the bottleneck that had been holding her back was her dining room table.

—

When you're done sorting the items in the room you're organizing, I suggest going through the rest of the home and gathering up any misplaced items that fit into one of the sections in that room.

—

For you, it might be your bed or even a small, underutilized closet. Once Holly learned to apply the primary principle of dividing things into sections, she was able to tackle the rest of the house, armed with a basic tool that made organizing sustainable for her and her family in the long term.

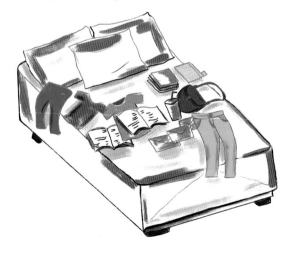

A more involved project I worked on was with Steve, a man in his forties going through a difficult divorce.

Steve had recently moved into a home where his two young daughters would also stay. When I first went to his house, everything was in chaos. There were piles of papers, children's toys and doll clothes, vinyl records, old cassettes, hundreds of books, and partially unpacked moving boxes, as well as his clothing and coats all over the house. There was no order to anything. Steve was totally overwhelmed and didn't know where to start.

The first thing I did with Steve's living room was to survey it all and identify what items were there, using a more general broad-brush sorting approach, rather than getting too specific. Then I pulled out my 8½-x-11-inch paper and pen and wrote down the sections I had identified. I taped each one to a part of the room where we could gather and sort those items. Many of the sections wouldn't end up in the living room in the end, but for the initial sort, we gathered and sorted the **children's toys, clothes, and books** in this area as we evaluated the whole house.

As we sorted, we realized his books needed further sorting. One group of books was in a special category because they were leather-bound classics—collector's items. Since these needed their own section, we set up an area in one corner of the room and labeled it "leather-bound classics." As we walked through other rooms in the house, we found several more leather-bound collector's books in various places. Over the course of the next several weeks, we grouped together dozens more books that would go in this section.

Many of the other books in the room were used more frequently. The ones Steve used most often were the science, history, and architecture books. We needed another section, which we called "current books." Not only were these two sections of distinctly different books, but they also needed to be

stored in two different areas. We determined that the leather-bound classics would be best suited to a glass-enclosed antique bookcase we found in another room. It was the perfect way to preserve the books, but keep them visible, since they were heirlooms with great sentimental value that had been handed down from his grandfather, and keep them accessible for the rare times he wanted to pull one out. The whole collection fit perfectly in one corner of the room.

In the current books section, we placed all the other books we found throughout the house, then organized them into more specific categories: architecture, history, science, and travel. As this section filled up, it became easier to decide on the best way to store these books. We determined that open shelving would work best, so Steve chose a

Pro Tip:

When sorting and you see things piling up, this is probably a good place for shelving. Take the piles as a sign that the location might be a convenient spot to store your items, only the shelving and containers are missing. Now that you have your items piled in plain view, you can consider what the shelves should look like and how they will function. Should they be tall shelves? Low shelves? Do you want doors on the shelves to conceal the contents? See Chapter Three for more on containers and other storage solutions.

color and style that he liked and did an online search to find just what he wanted. At this point, we had a good idea of how many books would be stored in this area, and we knew the sizes of the books he wanted to store, so we were able to choose the right shelving, allowing extra room for his growing collection.

>> mini Tip: When magazines pile up, apply the rule of "current and next." Keep the current month and next month's issue and toss or recycle the previous months. If you tend to collect magazines or other printed materials, clip just the articles you are interested in and create an "articles to read" file, rather than keeping the whole issue, and toss the source.

As you can see from this example, the "containerizing" of a section of items should ideally be the last thing you do. It's never a good idea to buy the bookcase first and then try to retrofit all the books into it. Of course, if you already own the bookcases, you can start by gathering all the books onto the shelves you have. We'll take a closer look at storage solutions in Chapter Three.

Among Steve's various books, there were piles of papers, boxes, envelopes, magazines, and newspapers. There were children's toys, little girl costumes, and small plastic shoes for playing dress-up. So, in one section of the room, I placed a sheet of paper on the wall that said "kids' toys," and in another, I created a section called "newspapers and magazines."

Once we had those sections clearly marked, the sorting process could continue. We added sections for "papers and enve-lopes" and for "music and DVDs." And so it went until we had the large room sorted into nearly a dozen smaller sections. As we continued to find more items—tools for small house repairs, art supplies for kids' projects, shoes, boots, and various jackets—we added labels, ending up with sections for "tools," "cleaning supplies," "art projects," "office supplies," and "clothing." The sections stayed like this for a while, while we searched the house to find all the items that would fit into each section.

>> mini TIP: Keep only what you use and love! This is easier to do after you have analyzed and sorted your things.

>> mini TIP: Sort what you have in front of you. If it belongs somewhere else, put it in a box so it doesn't distract you from the task at hand. When you are done, take it where it belongs.

Pro Tip:

Many clients I've worked with want to spend all day on Saturday organizing, but professional organizers know that after three or four hours, you are no longer as productive, and you risk burnout when you go beyond that time frame. Plan on three to four hours max per session when working on your own.

If you do plan to spend a whole day on your organizing project, fit in a two-hour break to change your focus and location. Take a walk on the beach, in a park, or around the neighborhood. Organizing involves a lot of close-up, detailed work, so do something that will take you out of that mindset and allow you to look into the distance.

Remember, when you work at a job for eight hours, you take a few breaks to have a cup of coffee or walk down the hallway. Organizing is not meant to be torture. You want to make it inspiring and fun!

The next step was to determine where the bottleneck was. How did Steve get into this predicament to begin with? Since I'm not a therapist, I wasn't going to analyze the factors that might have been underlying the situation. However, I know enough about human nature and my own personal growth process to know that *whatever emotional issues a person is dealing with, the physical manifestation is usually the last thing that changes.* Part of my job is to support my clients through this phase of their journey and transformation.

As I looked around, I realized that the bottleneck in this house was the basement. It was a large, spacious area filled with items from various categories of Steve's former married life that he had been putting off sorting. The energy in the basement was stuck and stagnant. Every surface was covered with books, supplies, clothes, toys, and cobwebs. The space had great potential but was maxed out with all sorts of items; not one more thing could be stored down there. Steve needed to take the big step of deciding what to keep and what to let go of to clear the bottleneck and move forward. If we could sort out that basement, we could create shelving all around the newly cleared space. This relief valve would then give us plenty of space to create the sections we needed and comfortably organize everything.

Once all your things have been gathered and divided up into their respective sections, it's time to closely examine what you have and decide what to keep, throw away, or donate. Keep what you love and use. This is also the time to be brutally honest with yourself about what you don't need and what isn't serving you. When in doubt, rest assured that someone out there in the world probably needs it more than you.

Any item that is not related to the sections you've established, but that you don't want to throw away or donate, can be removed and placed in a holding area in a box. This way, you avoid getting caught up in "paralysis by analysis" and spending a lot of time making minor decisions. You can go back and sort and analyze the items in the holding area box later.

Once you have a handle on distinct sections and have removed all the items you're planning to toss or donate, it's time to go back to the first question: What activities do you want to do in this room?

In Steve's case, he knew he wanted to read and watch TV in the living room and wanted the children to be able to play there as well. So, we knew we needed a place for the TV, a couch and chairs, bookcases, and a box for children's toys. Use your own answer to this question to guide you as you set up your furniture and move on to the next basic principle: creating zones.

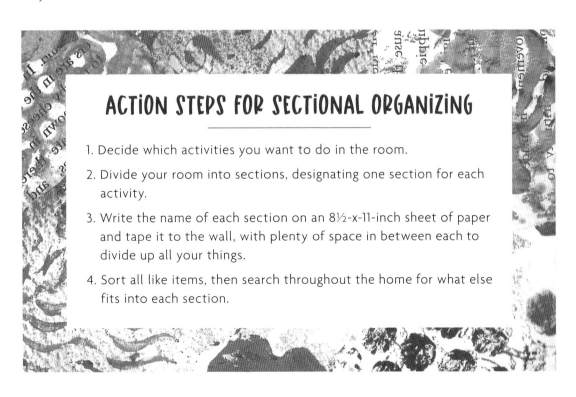

ACTION STEPS FOR SECTIONAL ORGANIZING

1. Decide which activities you want to do in the room.

2. Divide your room into sections, designating one section for each activity.

3. Write the name of each section on an 8½-x-11-inch sheet of paper and tape it to the wall, with plenty of space in between each to divide up all your things.

4. Sort all like items, then search throughout the home for what else fits into each section.

Chapter Two

ZONES

Organizing and purging is a way of making peace with the past and allowing yourself to move on.

ZONES

THE SECOND PRIMARY PRINCIPLE—REPRESENTED BY YELLOW IN OUR COLOR WHEEL—IS

ESTABLISHING
ZONES

Zones are a way of prioritizing the stuff you have within each section of a room and deciding what to keep and where to put it.

HOW MANY TIMES have you walked into a room in your home, perhaps the office or a bedroom, looking for something specific, but in the process, you find your sixteen-year-old daughter's baby rattle or a pile of baby photos, and the next thing you know, you're sitting there going down memory lane? When these things happen, it's time to think about zones. Organizing and purging are a way to make peace with the past, decide what is worth keeping, and move forward and enjoy your life.

In Chapter One, we learned how to define the sections of a room. But within each section, whatever is currently most essential to you should be right at your fingertips. I came up with the zones principle because many people make the mistake of assigning equal importance to all objects in a room. It is important to give top priority to the objects that you use often—they should be in the most convenient place, which is zone 1. Objects that you use less often should be in zone 2 or 3.

—

> It is important to give top priority to the objects that you use often— they should be in the most convenient place, which is zone 1.

—

When I get to a client's home or office, I usually find all sorts of items collected as if they were all equally important. There might be a current calendar along with calendars from the past five or six years. There might be tax records dating back ten or more years and a lifetime's worth of family photos. Applying the zones principle means deciding which of these items you need easily accessible, which you want to keep but don't need to access regularly, and which you may not need at all. When my clients use this method, they can gain significant space in their living areas, because older, less-used items can be stored somewhere else.

Remember Steve, who sorted everything in his house into appropriate sections? Before he could begin to put it all away, he needed to determine which zone it belonged in. For example, Steve had hundreds of books in his current books section. As he reviewed them one more time, he evaluated which books he wanted to access most often. These would be stored in the living room, which would be his zone 1 for current books. Books that didn't make it into zone 1 but that Steve still wanted to access somewhat regularly would go in zone 2, which we decided would be a small bookcase in his bedroom. Finally, we assigned a zone 3, which would be in the basement on another set of bookshelves. The books in zone 3 were books Steve had already read that he wanted to keep but didn't necessarily need to have in the living room.

—

> I took advantage of the high ceilings and stacked milk crates to give me more space.

—

I started thinking about zones when I lived in a 6-x-10-foot dorm room in college in New York City. I had all of my stuff right next to me, and there just wasn't enough space for everything. I was an art student, and I had art supplies, clothes for dressing up and dressing down, books, and homework supplies. I took advantage of the high ceilings and stacked milk crates to give me more space, then organized my belongings. The things I used most often, such as my in-season clothes and my current semester's art supplies, went into zone 1 in my bedroom closet and the drawers below. Zone 2 items, like out-of-season clothes and the art supplies I wasn't currently using, were also stored in my room, but I kept them in milk crates stacked high above the closet. And I had a small art studio

—

This might seem obvious, but if one or more of your zone 1 items is missing from your desk, you will be inturrupted and have to get up and look for it.

—

down the hall, which became zone 3, where I would store all my extra art supplies, school supplies, and bulky items like my boots and coats or any extra out-of-season clothes.

Let's look at how you can apply the zones principle to set up your desk area or home office.

ZONE ONE

Zone 1 items are the items you want to have at your fingertips—the items you use the most frequently or that are the most important to you. Put these right on your desk. Of course, that means your computer and basic supplies. It should also include your most relevant files, which are best placed in a step-file sorter for easy access. You will also

want to include your calendar, whether it's on your phone or a desktop version, and any other items you reach for daily.

This might seem obvious, but if one or more of your zone 1 items is missing from your desk, you will be interrupted and have to get up to look for it. Every time you leave your desk to hunt for the scissors or tape, you are inevitably distracted by other things. This will only make you more disorganized because you don't have the chance to finish the original task at hand.

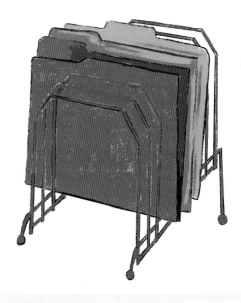

>> mini TIP: Use an incline file sorter, (AKA step-file sorter) in the zone 1 area of your desk for your "fingertip" files. These are the files that relate to projects you are currently working on and that you use every day.

ZONE ONE SUPPLY LIST FOR YOUR HOME OFFICE

While this is not an exhaustive list, most people will need some or all of the following in their zone 1 desk area:

- ⊘ SCISSORS
- ⊘ PENS THAT WORK
- ⊘ SHARPENED PENCILS
- ⊘ RULER
- ⊘ STAPLER
- ⊘ PAPER CLIPS/BINDER CLIPS

- ⊘ TAPE
- ⊘ STICKY NOTES
- ⊘ PAPER
- ⊘ STAMPS
- ⊘ FREQUENTLY USED FILES

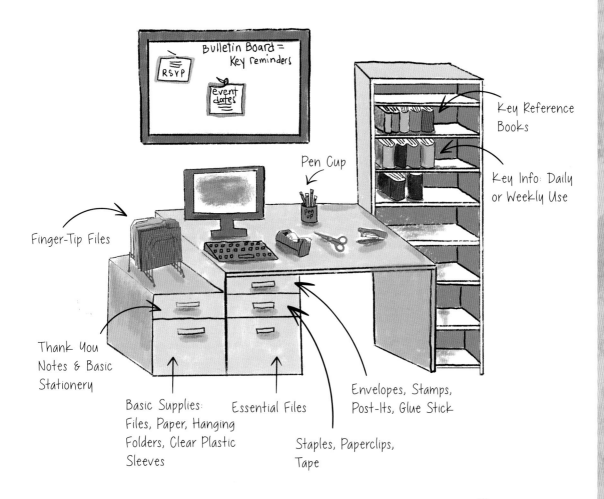

Bulletin Board = Key reminders

RSVP

event dates

Pen Cup

Key Reference Books

Key Info: Daily or Weekly Use

Finger-Tip Files

Thank You Notes & Basic Stationery

Basic Supplies: Files, Paper, Hanging Folders, Clear Plastic Sleeves

Essential Files

Staples, Paperclips, Tape

Envelopes, Stamps, Post-Its, Glue Stick

ZONE TWO

Zone 2 items are the items you use somewhat regularly, but not as often as the zone 1 items. These could include reference books or notebooks that you refer to from time to time but don't need every day. Your zone 2 items should be kept nearby, but don't need to be right at your fingertips. For example, you might store them in a cabinet behind your desk.

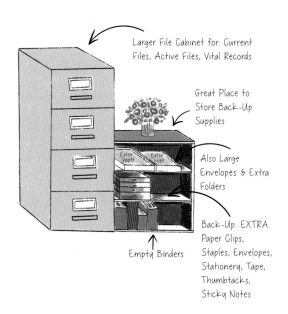

Larger File Cabinet for: Current Files, Active Files, Vital Records

Great Place to Store Back-Up Supplies

Also Large Envelopes & Extra Folders

Back-Up...EXTRA: Paper Clips, Staples, Envelopes, Stationery, Tape, Thumbtacks, Sticky Notes

Empty Binders

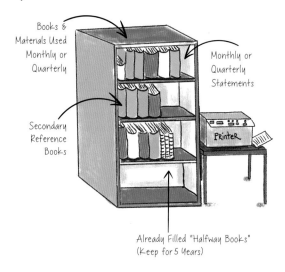

Books & Materials Used Monthly or Quarterly

Monthly or Quarterly Statements

Secondary Reference Books

Printer

Already Filled "Halfway Books" (Keep for 5 Years)

ZONE 3 ITEMS = Items you only need to access on occasion.

ZONE 2 ITEMS = Items used less frequently, either monthly or quarterly.

ZONE THREE

Zone 3 is for the items you don't need to have within arm's reach, such as extra office supplies or older files. A closet or shelf might be a good place for these items. You'll have to get up out of your chair to go retrieve them, so zone 3 is for items you only need to access on occasion.

ZONE FOUR

Depending on the room, you may need a zone 4 for items that are important enough to keep, but that you don't need to access often. In organizing your desk, this might include things like old tax records or old medical records. You can put your zone 4 items high up in a closet, where they'll be out of reach, but you'll know where they are if you should ever need them. In other rooms, zone 4 items might include outgrown children's clothes that you are saving as keepsakes or to give to the next baby, valued memorabilia, or items you use only once a year, like ski clothes and equipment. These can be stored in the attic or basement. (Note: be sure to check which items need to be stored in a controlled climate.)

Occasionally, people have a zone 5, like an off-site storage facility or the upper rafters of a garage, attic, or basement. This can be helpful for items of sentimental value that rarely, if ever, need to be accessed, like old journals or family heirlooms, but I generally discourage it. Use a zone 5 only if absolutely necessary, because once they're stored, these items will rarely be seen again.

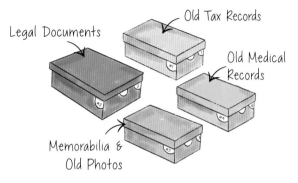

Inventory Sheet
1) Old Tax Records
2) Legal Documents
3) Memorabilia & Old Photos
4) Old Medical Records

Old Tax Records
Legal Documents
Old Medical Records
Memorabilia & Old Photos

ZONE 4 ITEMS = Items important enough to keep, but that you don't need access too often.

>> **mini TIP:** What you keep in zone 4 or 5 is a matter of quantity. Ask yourself, "How much of this do I really need or want to keep?"

• • •

I used the zones principle to help one of my clients, Stacy, who I had first worked with when her son, Jeff, was about eight years old.

At that time, he still had a little boy's room filled with toys, stuffed animals, clothes, and games. We used the sections principle to determine the right spot for each activity, then found the right containers for each section.

I went back to work with Jeff six years later, when he was fourteen. The sorting process was more customized this time since now he had his own opinions about where things should go and what he wanted to keep, toss, or donate. Before we began the sorting, he had games, sports equipment, and

a few stuffed animals on or near his desk. We cleared the desktop as well as the drawers to set up a clear and usable zone 1 for him.

Before we applied the zones principle, all his papers, artwork, and stuffed animals were taking up equal importance in his space. When I explained the zone principle, he quickly sorted what he wanted on his desk in zone 1. After much discussion, he decided he was okay with letting go of most of the stuffed animals, some of which had been in his room for fourteen years. He was able to

ZONES 37

prioritize the "best of" and gently say goodbye to the rest. We removed all the papers he had in his desk that dated back to first grade and gave all the "best of" artwork and papers to his mom to store in a memorabilia box. He had also collected computer motherboards to take apart when he was younger, but now realized he wasn't into that anymore. He kept one or two and got rid of the rest that were clogging up his desk drawers.

Now there was room to have hanging folders in his drawer, and we labeled them by the class subjects he was taking. We found a great spot above his new teenage bed to add a shelf for his favorite stuffed animals, and we donated toys and games that he had outgrown.

For the clothes in his room, I designed a closet that would suit his needs. I added more shelves than drawers because he told me that he frequently threw things into drawers and couldn't find them again. We realized that due to his school's dress code, he needed plenty of hanging space for jackets and button-down shirts. His room now looked more like a teenager's room, with plenty of floor space to hang out and relax.

• • •

Another client of mine, Pamela, was a single mom who had a large kitchen but complained that she didn't have room for any of her cooking supplies.

We opened every cabinet and found a lot of kid materials taking up space. There were water bottles, sports equipment, and things for the kids' lunches mixed in with Pamela's baking supplies. In her case, the

—

Ask yourself which kitchen items you actually use and put the rest in a less prominent holding area for the one or two times a year you might need them.

—

water bottles, snacks for sports, and lunch boxes were used daily and needed to be in their own zone 1. Many of the baking materials were used far less often. There were also duplicate mixing bowls and measuring cups taking up space, and Pamela told me she really only used three or four of her pots and pans. So, we created a zone 2 space for the items that were used a little less frequently and put the rest of the baking items in a zone 3 section in the basement for occasional use.

Pamela had three full sets of dishes stored in the kitchen: one for everyday use, one that had been her grandmother's, and one that had been given to her when she got married. We moved the fancy set that had been her grandmother's from the kitchen to the cabinet in the dining room, and we moved the gift set to zone 3, so it was there if she had a large party and needed more dishes.

Ask yourself which kitchen items you actually use and put the rest in a less prominent holding area for the one or two times a year you might need them. This way, you'll always know where your holiday cooking items are, but they won't get in your way daily.

• • •

Another client of mine, Cathy, lived in a one-bedroom apartment.

She was an artist and thought of everything as having equal importance in her small space. But when we started talking, it turned out she never ate in her kitchen, because the kitchen had the best light and she liked to create her art there.

The kitchen had shelves that were taken up with a bread maker, a mixer, and a juicer, all of which she used only rarely. Her art supplies, meanwhile, were in a closet nowhere near where she liked to work. We rearranged things so that the supplies she used every day were in her zone 1—in this case, on a middle shelf in the kitchen. We moved the mixer and juicer to a bottom shelf and moved the bread maker, which she only used when her grandson visited, to the closet. We also moved all her oversized pots,

A ROOM SET UP WITH ZONES 1–3

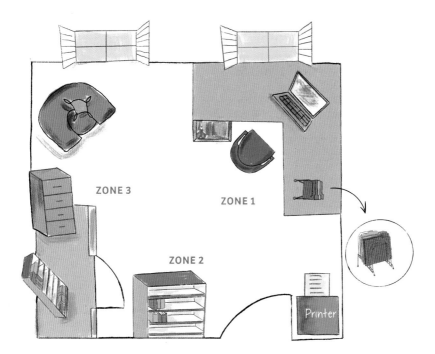

ZONE 3

ZONE 1

ZONE 2

Printer

which she only used for cooking once-in-a-while meals like lobster and turkey, to zone 3, in the closet on a high shelf.

In her bedroom, Cathy wanted a bookcase and a place to read, but there was stuff everywhere that didn't seem to fit anywhere in the house, like luggage and piles of books. We put risers under her bed to lift her bed frame two inches so she could store all the luggage under her bed. Once the luggage was removed, she had space for a bookcase. She moved her art books onto the shelves in the kitchen, in zone 1 next to her art supplies, because that's where she would use them. All her other books could now be stored in her bedroom.

• • •

Taking time to establish what belongs in each zone will improve your productivity and help you really make a space of your own.

This reminds me of a client I had recently who was going through a transition in her life and her physical space. When I first met Catherine, she was a professor at a prestigious

—

First, I asked her what activities she envisioned doing there.

—

university and had been teaching for nearly twenty-five years. She was in her early sixties and was about to retire. She was considering taking on a small project or two in her profession, but she primarily wanted to explore other things, like the arts and teaching yoga. When I arrived at her home, she showed me the guest room that she wanted to transform into her new sanctuary and small office.

First, I asked her what activities she envisioned doing there. Meditation was one, and she also enjoyed creating artwork in different mediums, including painting on paper, which was mostly new to her, and creating wire sculptures with gemstones. She wanted some desk space for working on papers and other small projects and needed a small area to shelve the textbooks and reference books she wanted to have on hand. She also wanted a section of the room for doing yoga.

There were a few obvious choices for the best locations for some of these activities based on where the best light was and where I could find some hidden storage spots. The first thing we needed to do was divide the room into sections. We came up with sections for "art," "meditation/yoga," and "desk/work." The room was about 280 square feet, which was plenty of room to work with. The one thing we knew for sure was that we were keeping a queen size bed in there for guests.

There was a comfy wingback chair that was perfect for her meditation section. On that chair, she hung a cozy blanket, and we placed a small table next to the chair for her zone 1 items related to meditation, including notebooks, her favorite healing crystals, and her iPad for meditative music. She could keep her yoga mat rolled up next to the chair and roll it right out in front of the chair when needed.

The next section we designated for artwork. Catherine wanted to spread out on the floor when she was creating art, so we needed a plan for where and how to store art supplies. There was a bookcase in this room that was perfect for many of her textbooks and reference books and still had room left over for some of her most frequently used art supplies—her zone 1 for art projects. The rest of the supplies needed to go somewhere else. I realized there was a closet in the back of the room. She said it

Pro Tip:

Make sure the space in which you store less frequently used items is sufficiently climate controlled. I've had clients open boxes to find their belongings covered with mold or eaten by moths or termites.

Store items in an airtight container. To help manage moths and moisture, try any of the following:

+ Dehumidifier rods for closets

+ Moth-Away sachets in pockets and tucked between folded clothing

+ Cedar blocks to repel moths

+ Sterilite clear gasket boxes to safeguard items from air and moisture

was like an attic space and was rarely used. That seemed like a perfect zone 2 storage solution for her art supplies! The small back room was a hidden gem for storage. We cleared some large pieces of luggage and some random boxes out of the way, and now we had a lot of space to work with. We found another small bookcase to put there for all her overflow art supplies, as well as her gemstones and related objects.

We made sure to have lots of extra lighting at Catherine's desk for her art projects and bought some bins with handles that she could store all the art supplies in and easily pull out when she was ready to work at her desk. This allowed her to store the stones and other supplies in an out-of-the-way zone

—

If the area of your home or office you are starting with has never had a comfortable flow, now is the time to establish one.

—

when not in use and made it all portable for when she was ready to work on her art projects.

Next, we considered where to place a "desk/work" section. The room had a bay window, which seemed like the best place to put a small desk. I also spotted two little doors on either side of the room, which I named the Alice in Wonderland doors. They were smaller than usual, maybe three feet tall. When I inquired about these, Catherine

said they were tiny closets she never used because they seemed so small and impractical. I was intrigued.

As soon as I opened the little closets, I saw great opportunity. In one we were able to fit a two-drawer file cabinet, which she used for her zone 2 files, keeping only zone 1 files in her desk. The other little closet was perfect for a small table to hold her printer with an extension cord run under the door. Getting those bulky items out of zone 1 made the desk area much more streamlined.

After setting up her space just as she needed, Catherine had a fabulous multiuse room she could call her sanctuary. She could still host guests from time to time and use the surface of the bed for projects that required her to spread out with papers. She was thrilled with her new room setup and felt ready to move into this new phase of her life!

If the area of your home or office you are starting with has never had a comfortable flow, now is the time to establish one. As you create your zones, think about what you

—

Surround yourself with all the things that make your heart sing yes, yes, yes!

—

really need to work in your space effectively. Do you want a desk and a sofa in that room, or do you prefer a reading chair? Do you need a lamp? How about a place to store supplies or backup items?

Also, ask yourself how you'd like each room to feel. Should it be relaxing or ener-gizing? A contemplative oasis or an efficient and streamlined workspace? Professional and minimalist or creative and artsy?

What are your favorite colors and inspiring images? Surround yourself with all the things that make your heart sing *yes, yes, yes!* Use a bulletin board or framed artwork to feature inspiring messages and images. Your home and workspaces should be inviting and comfortable. From the desk to the chair, to the supplies, to the storage and lighting, it's important that your spaces reflect what inspires you and gives you the sense that you belong there—that you feel a sense of connection and a desire to be there.

• • •

Several years ago, I worked for a family of five in New York City.

Carla and Dan had three daughters, and I first worked with Lisa, who was thirteen at the time. We had so much fun turning her room into her personal refuge. Lisa was having a hard time in school and had been struggling with attention deficit disorder. When I first walked into her room, it looked like a hurricane had come through! Clothes were all over the floor, and schoolbooks and papers were everywhere. Her bathroom was a total mess, and her closet was overflowing with stuff she had had since she was a little girl. She had trophies and awards here and there, but you couldn't see them unless you rummaged through everything. She seemed quite shy and embarrassed about her room. I had the sense that she felt ashamed and overwhelmed.

—

When I first walked into her room, it looked like a hurricane had come through!

—

As we began working together, I asked her what kinds of things she liked to do. As it turned out, she was an excellent swimmer and had won many awards and medals at swimming competitions. She loved surfing as well as fashion and dressing up. She had lots of good friends and loved going to the theater with her mom.

As we began sorting what was in her room, we came up with clear sections, and little by little, week after week, I began to see Lisa come out of her shell. We designated sections of her room for:

- ⊘ **Proudly displaying her swim trophies and medals**
- ⊘ **Storing schoolbooks and supplies**
- ⊘ **Getting ready for school in the morning**
- ⊘ **Surfing memorabilia and décor**
- ⊘ **Her social life and friends**
- ⊘ **Clothes**

Once we'd defined the sections, Lisa sorted through her things using the zones principle. For example, in the getting-ready section, she stored basic toiletries and everything she needed to blow-dry and style her hair front and center, in front of the mirror above her dresser. In her closet, we created a section for the clothes she really liked and wanted to keep, we then organized these garments by type and length.

I brought my label maker and taught her how to use it. Having things labeled can be a huge relief: now, Lisa didn't have to wonder if she was "doing it right" when it came time to put things away. She knew exactly where everything went because her drawers and shelves were clearly labeled.

By the time we got the whole room organized, she was so happy and proud to invite her friends over to her house and into her room. She grew much more self-confident, and her bubbly personality began to shine through.

Sorting through your belongings and organizing your space by defining sections, then prioritizing the items in each section into zones to decide what's truly important to you, can be enormously empowering. But there's one last primary key to keeping a space well-organized and easy to use: finding the right storage solutions. We'll tackle those in the next chapter.

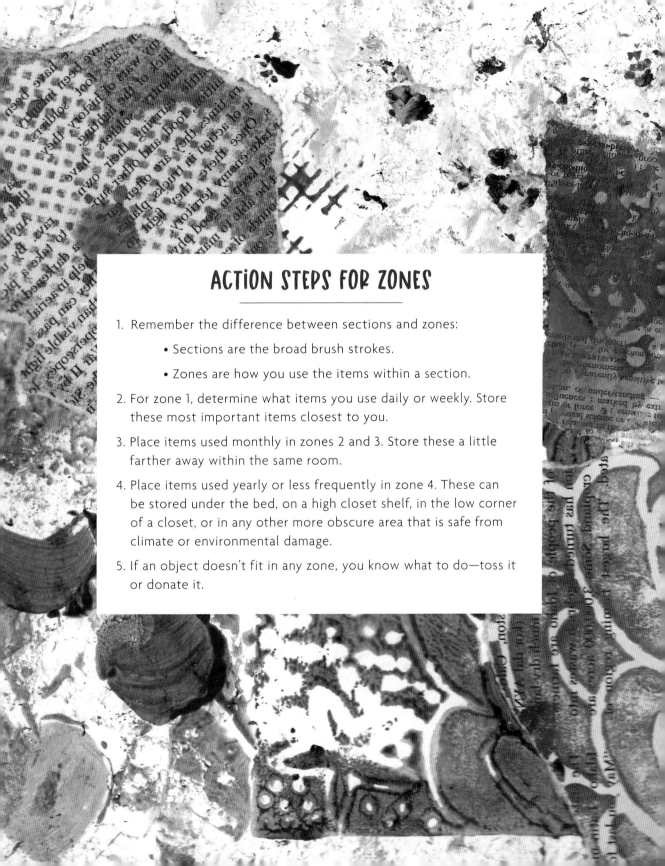

ACTION STEPS FOR ZONES

1. Remember the difference between sections and zones:
   - Sections are the broad brush strokes.
   - Zones are how you use the items within a section.
2. For zone 1, determine what items you use daily or weekly. Store these most important items closest to you.
3. Place items used monthly in zones 2 and 3. Store these a little farther away within the same room.
4. Place items used yearly or less frequently in zone 4. These can be stored under the bed, on a high closet shelf, in the low corner of a closet, or in any other more obscure area that is safe from climate or environmental damage.
5. If an object doesn't fit in any zone, you know what to do—toss it or donate it.

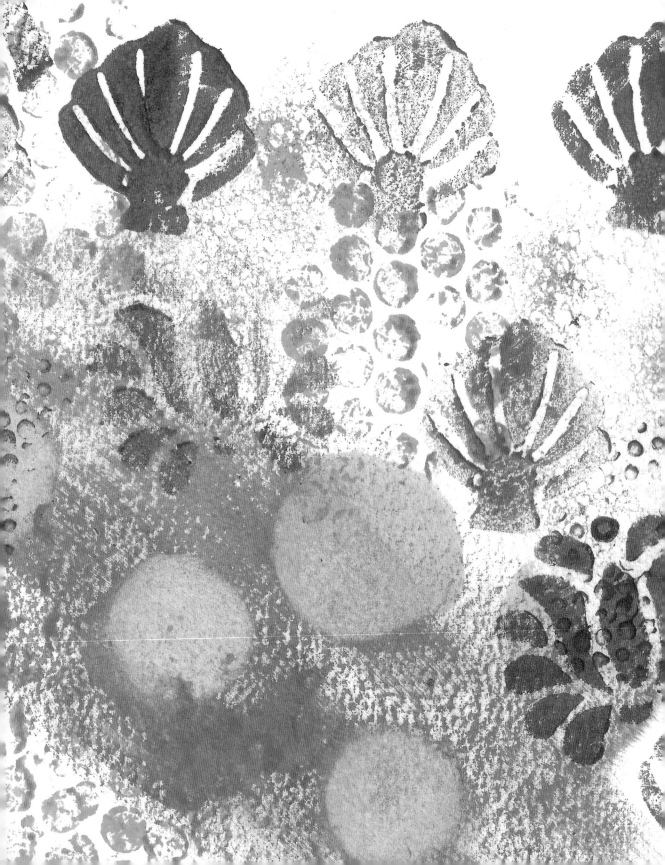

Chapter Three

STORAGE SOLUTIONS

"The ability to simplify means to eliminate the unnecessary so that the necessary may speak."
—HANS HOFMANN

STORAGE
SOLUTIONS

3

THE NEXT AND FINAL PRIMARY PRINCIPLE—REPRESENTED BY BLUE IN OUR COLOR WHEEL—IS

STORAGE SOLUTIONS

Once you've successfully divided your space into sections and prioritized your things using the zones principle, the next and final primary step is finding the right storage solutions for each section and zone in your home.

BY NOW, YOU SHOULD HAVE a good sense of how the first two primary principles of organizing can help you redesign your space in a way that's practical and perfectly suited to your needs. But of course, no organizational system is complete without the right storage solutions.

I can't tell you how many times I have arrived at a client's home or office and heard them say, "I bought all these great organizing and storage containers. I don't know why I can't get organized!" The problem with this approach is that no matter how attractive or functional your storage containers are, they won't help you get organized unless they're

> A lot of people hear the word *storage* and think about the basement, the garage, or the closets, but storage is everywhere, in every room.

the right containers for your specific needs. All those pretty things out there are designed to lure you in, but the smartest way to shop is to first determine exactly what you want to store and how you're going to use or retrieve these items. Only then should you set out to find something that will fit your needs. When you create an organizing system that's customized to work for you, it frees up the mental energy you need to be more creative and lets your thoughts flow more freely.

A lot of people hear the word *storage* and think about the basement, the garage, or the closets, but storage is everywhere, in every room. When we talk about storage, first we want to look at the items we're storing, then we want to think about zones, as discussed in Chapter Two, then we can talk

about the ideal container for each item. For example, if an item is frequently used, it is a zone 1 item, which means it should be stored at your fingertips or at the point of use. So, you'll want to choose a storage container that keeps that item easily accessible.

Let's review a few basic concepts and then go into a little more detail. First, remember that everything must have a home! And if you want to be able to use an item regularly, you'll need to keep two things in mind:

- ⊘ **Always store for retrieval—make sure you know where to find it.**

- ⊘ **Store it where you can reach it and ideally where you can see at least part of it.**

I suggest that you label all containers so everyone in your household can understand and follow the same system. If you are sharing a space with a spouse or significant other, it's important to explain what you're doing and get their input as you create the system. If the other person doesn't like where you want to store the toilet paper, for example, then you need to rethink where it's going to be stored. A household system will only function well if you have everyone's buy-in.

Once you've figured out what items you need to store, think about how you'd like to access them before you head out to buy the pretty containers. Would these items fit better in drawers or on shelves? Should they go in bins or baskets? If you're buying storage boxes, should they have lids or not? Do you prefer wood containers or plastic? If plastic, should they be clear, so you can see what's inside, or a solid color, to hide the contents? Do your storage solutions need to be portable or stationary? In a living room, for example, you may want open shelving to feature all your books, family photos, and prized vacation mementos, but you may prefer solid-colored, labeled bins to neatly corral your kids' toys. All the storage solutions mentioned in this chapter can be found at The Container Store, on Amazon, or through the Häfele website. There is a wide range of price points available for each type of product. Whichever you choose, the key is to take good measurements before you shop.

Now, let's look at how you can put these principles into practice to choose the right storage for any type of room. Let's begin with two rooms that always have a lot of zone 1 items, plus overflow items: the kitchen and the bathroom.

THE KITCHEN

The kitchen is one of the busiest rooms in the house, so it's essential that it functions well. As always, you want whatever you use frequently to be in zone 1, as close as possible to the place where you use it. For example, you'll need a storage solution for

your drinking glasses close to the fridge, you'll want your everyday dishes close to the table for easy table setting or close to where you are cooking and serving, and you'll want to store pots and pans near the stove. Don't store duplicate kitchen gadgets. Do you really need three vegetable peelers? Maybe not. Keep your favorite and donate the rest.

Shelf extenders are a great way to add more storage space in a small kitchen. Large, cavernous cabinets can easily become cluttered and disorganized when there isn't enough shelving. Shelf extenders maximize the usable space inside the cabinets so you can see everything and access it easily. The goal with any space is to make better use of the height, so you're not wasting valuable vertical space. But you don't want to end up with stacks of items that are impossible to access. Before you shop for shelf extenders, take precise measurements of your cabinet

UNDER-SINK PULL-OUT RACKS

and the items you're planning to store in them. This way you know how much space you have to work with and can buy the appropriate shelf extenders.

I also recommend adding pull-out racks beneath the kitchen sink and installing pull-

out shelves in all lower cabinets. This makes life much easier than having to bend down and dig deep inside stationary shelving. If replacing your shelves with pull-outs isn't possible, for example, if you are renting your home or you are on a tight budget, use open boxes on your lower shelves or get clear plastic or metal mesh drawers that are the depth of your cabinet. This gives you the convenience of a pull-out rack without having to make any permanent changes. I recommend plastic or metal because they are easy to wipe clean when needed. Woven baskets, however, collect crumbs inside the weave and make it more difficult to clean.

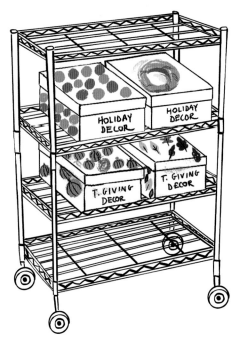

When it comes to storing larger, awkward kitchen items like your food processor, blender, slow cooker and toaster oven, one solution is a rolling cart with shelves that can be pushed into a corner when not in use. I've even seen one of these used for a small tabletop dishwasher that was wheeled next to the sink when needed so that the hose could be attached to a sink faucet! It's much neater to collect all these large items in one place rather than having them placed randomly all over the kitchen counters taking up valuable workspace.

Remember to think about the zones principle before you choose your storage containers. If your sink only gets clogged up once a year, you don't need the Drano in zone 1, but perhaps you'll need a bin to hold it and other related items in a zone 3 or 4 closet or cabinet. That pretty bowl from your grandmother and the wine glasses you only use when company comes over may belong in a zone 3 cabinet in the dining room. Duplicate items that you don't want to get rid of and holiday items that you use only once a year could go into a zone 4—perhaps a special shelf in the basement or garage designated for holiday items. Make sure to place these zone 4 items in labeled boxes so you know where to find them when the holidays roll around.

MESSY DRAWER VS ORGANIZED DRAWER

You can also store items like this in the pantry, if space permits, or look around your kitchen for a rarely used space and consider storing your frequently used appliances there. For example, I had a client who stored her toaster oven inside a larger oven in her kitchen. She had two ovens and almost never used the second one, so it became the perfect place to store a bulky appliance. If you use a space like this for storage, just be sure to label it clearly, so everyone in

your household knows not to use that oven without checking inside first.

Finally, there is the all-too-popular "junk drawer." If it's junk, why are you keeping it? It is helpful to designate one drawer in the kitchen as a central supply drawer—you will often need scissors, a tape measure, pens, a pad of paper, and scotch tape, for example. But if it's not something you use regularly, it doesn't belong in your central supply drawer.

Once you've eliminated the junk and gathered the items you really need in your supply drawer, buy the right size inserts to help keep it neat. Before shopping for inserts, be sure to measure the interior dimensions of your drawer (the usable space). I recommend purchasing individual drawer organizers in wood, bamboo, or white. Clear drawer inserts are not as effective, because they can make the drawer look just as disorganized as it did without the inserts.

THE PANTRY

The ideal pantry setup is to have large, but not deep, pull-out shelves, so you can group like items together on individual shelves. Label each shelf so all family members can follow the system. For example, you might have one whole pull-out shelf for "savory snacks" and another for "sweet snacks."

If pull-out shelves aren't possible, I suggest using side-by-side open boxes to gather categories of food together in the pantry. It's okay if your pantry boxes are clear plastic; what's most important is that you group all like items together and label your boxes clearly in large letters on the front so that it's easy for everyone to find what they need. Your categories may vary depending on your individual household's habits and

In this cabinet, each lazy Susan has a theme: the top left one contains sweet spices and condiments, the top right holds all the hot and spicy items, and the two-tiered one on the bottom left contains all other herbs and spices. This cabinet uses the zones principle to place the most-used items at eye level with the less frequently used zone 2 spices higher up.

preferences, but the boxes could include categories such as savory snacks, sweet treats, pasta and rice, soups, condiments, canned goods, and so on.

If your shelves are stationary, and especially if you are using shelves that are higher than eye level, a lazy Susan is a great way to maximize your space. Items like canned goods and bottles that get pushed to the back of a shelf tend to get lost and forgotten, so grouping these items on a lazy Susan makes it easy to see what you have stored and reach what you need. Lazy Susans are also the most efficient way to store spices, condiments, vitamins and medicines; you can even use them in the fridge to prevent things from getting lost in the back and ending up as unintentional science experiments!

WHAT TO TOSS OR DONATE

- ⊘ OUTDATED OR BROKEN APPLIANCES
- ⊘ DUPLICATES OF ANYTHING YOU DON'T USE
- ⊘ PLASTIC STORAGE CONTAINERS WITHOUT MATCHING LIDS

- ⊘ CRACKED OR CHIPPED CHINA
- ⊘ LEAKY TRAVEL MUGS
- ⊘ WARPED POTS OR PANS
- ⊘ SCRATCHED NONSTICK POTS OR PANS
- ⊘ EXPIRED PANTRY ITEMS

- ⊘ OLD HERBS AND SPICES THAT HAVE LOST THEIR FLAVOR OR SCENT
- ⊘ OLD COFFEE BEANS
- ⊘ STAINED DISH TOWELS AND OVEN MITTS
- ⊘ HALF-USED CANDLES

Other items you might want to store in the pantry include paper goods, lightbulbs, batteries, and other household items. Again, the key is to corral like items together and place them in open-top boxes with clear, easy-to-read labels. For duplicate items, like multiple rolls of toilet paper or boxes of tissues, store one behind the other, like they are displayed in the grocery store. That way, you can see exactly what you have and there's no mystery about what's hiding behind the front item.

Another important point to remember in the pantry is to keep everything off the floor. I am a real stickler for cleanliness, especially in the pantry. If you have something that absolutely must remain on the floor, such as a bucket of cleaning supplies, make sure it's in an easy-to-move container so you can clean under or behind it. For more tips on storing cleaning supplies, see the Utility section on page 63.

THE BATHROOM

The next busiest room of the house—as well as one of the most crowded with the need to store a lot of items per square inch—is the bathroom. Ideally, you'd walk into the bathroom and always know where to find your tweezers, your razor, your Band-Aids, etc. But because bathrooms sometimes have limited storage, people often stash their toiletries wherever they will fit. Unfortunately, this means that when they need something, they don't know where to look for those items. A better solution is to assign a specific home for everything so you can find things in the same place every time.

One of the best tools for zone 1 storage in the bathroom is plastic stacking drawers divided by category, such as first aid, prescriptions, allergy and cold medicines, eye care, nail care, dental care, body products, makeup, etc. Ideally, place only one or two categories of

If there are multiple people sharing one bathroom, assign each member of the family a different towel rack or hook to hang wet towels to avoid confusion. You can also assign each person their own toiletries bucket or bag to keep in their bedroom and use to tote grooming supplies to and from the bathroom each morning, to make life easier and avoid clutter.

items in each drawer, grouping related items together *(for example, you might choose to store eye care, soap, makeup, razors, dental items, first-aid, and cold and allergy meds)*. Think about putting backup items, like extra toilet paper or soap, into a zone 2 or 3, which could be in a closet or pantry.

If you have built-in drawers, you can buy drawer dividers sized to meet your storage needs, or you can recycle various sizes of gift boxes to achieve the same effect.

This is a great way to recycle pretty packaging. If your cabinet doesn't have drawers, you can purchase clear plastic drawers to store under the sink. If there is no under-sink cabinet, you can attach fabric around the sink and hide your drawers underneath or buy a small cabinet to place in the bathroom or on the wall.

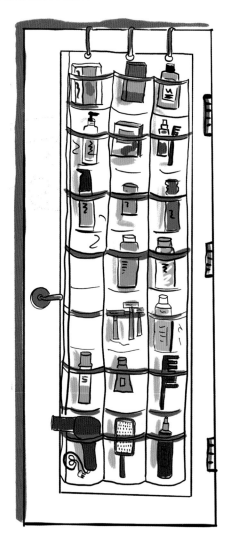

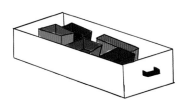

WHAT TO TOSS OR DONATE

- ⊘ EXPIRED MEDICINE, SUNSCREEN, AND TOILETRIES
- ⊘ ANY CREAMS OR LOTIONS THAT HAVE SEPARATED
- ⊘ NAIL POLISH THAT HAS SEPARATED
- ⊘ RIPPED OR STAINED TOWELS
- ⊘ MAKEUP THAT SMELLS STRANGE OR HAS CHANGED COLOR
- ⊘ APPLIANCES WITH WORN OR FRAYED CORDS

Another useful item in a bathroom is a clear shoe bag to hang behind a door. These are useful for organizing so much more than shoes—in the bathroom, you can use one to store bottles of toiletries, your hairdryer, brushes, combs, razors, etc.

Now that we've reviewed two of the busiest rooms in the house, let's examine storage solutions for a few more traditional storage spaces, including closets, attics, and basements.

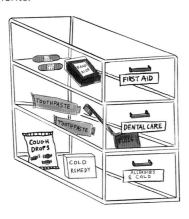

PRO TIPS:

* Use a liquid hand soap dispenser near all the sinks in the home! They are easy to fill and there is less mess.

* Thoroughly clean and organize your bathroom once a year to maintain the system and keep toiletries up to date. Follow this simple rule: when in doubt, throw it out.

* If you enjoy reading in your new-found "sanctuary," find an attractive container, such as an upright basket, for storing magazines. It is best to store magazines standing upright, not in a horizontal stack, so it's easy to flip through them and choose the magazine or catalog you want. Always save the current and next months' issues and toss older ones.

* Measuring for stackable drawers under the sink is essential. Take careful and accurate measurements of your usable space and stack, stack, stack your drawers. Put one or two categories of items in each box and label them! You will be amazed at how much you can store this way and how easily you can find things.

CLOSETS

Closets are the first thing most people think of when they hear the word *storage*. Whatever type of closet space you have in your home, it is important to think about how all the closets can work in relation to each other to create a successful whole-house organizational system. The most common closet spaces that we'll focus on are:

⊘ **Clothes closets**

⊘ **Linen closets**

⊘ **Entryway closets**

⊘ **Utility closets**

If your closet space is limited, you can create more storage space in a room by adding a rolling rack for hanging items. Use an attractive fabric, such as a pretty bedsheet or oversized tablecloth, to conceal the rolling rack from view if necessary. A freestanding wardrobe is another option, but these can be bulky and take up a lot of room. If you do have the space, finding the right wardrobe can be a fun way to add some character to your room's décor.

Clothes Closets

All clothing closets need shelving and at least one hanging rod. Whether they're wooden shelves or wire racks, having multiple shelves will help you keep things organized. If your closets lack shelving, you can stack plastic drawers of various sizes to store smaller items. If you have a closet with lots of hanging rods but not as many shelves, you can add stacked wood or metal mesh cubbies beneath the hanging rods to create compartmentalized storage. Regardless of how you create your shelves, you'll always want some bins or pull-out drawers for smaller items like socks, underwear, sleepwear, swimsuits, etc. If, on the other hand, your closet has more drawer storage than shelf or hanging space, you can add drawer dividers to help keep smaller items organized.

To begin organizing your closet, first divide your clothing into like groups (shirts, pants, dresses, etc.), and then sort each group of items into categories. For example, your shirts might be sorted into categories like:

⊘ **Long-sleeved shirts**

⊘ **Short-sleeved shirts**

⊘ **Evening shirts**

⊘ **Work shirts**

⊘ **Weekend shirts**

Do the same for your pants, skirts, shorts, and so on. I also suggest keeping all your workout clothes together in one area.

Once your clothes are categorized, you'll be able to choose the right layout and storage solutions for your needs. Store your clothing sorted by type and then by color;

for example, hanging all your short-sleeved shirts together, organized by color, then all your long-sleeved shirts together, also sorted by color. Keep the categories of clothing you wear most often front and center, so you can

—

Once your clothes are categorized, you'll be able to choose the right layout and storage solutions for your needs.

—

easily find the outfit you need each day, and try to keep as many items as possible visible so it's easy to identify what you have.

Whether to hang or fold items like shirts is a matter of fabric, type, and structure of your closet: Blouses and tops that have special details are best suited to hanging, while t-shirts should ideally be folded and stacked in low piles on a shelf so that you can identify them by the folded side that's facing out. Don't make your piles so high that they tip over when you pull a shirt out. You may want to make separate piles for different categories, such as such as short-sleeved and long-sleeved shirts. If you must keep your folded items in a drawer rather than on open shelves, it is much harder to keep them organized and see what's underneath the top layer. One way to help alleviate this is to fan the shirts out slightly from front to back as you stack one shirt on top of the next. Or, you can fold each shirt into a little roll or bundle and place

them one next to the other. (This style of folding should be a last resort if you have no shelving space and plenty of drawers because it takes a lot of discipline to keep up with folding your clothes into neat little rolls.)

Ideally, you want to use your drawers for smaller items that need to be grouped together, such as underwear, socks, bras, swimsuits, and workout clothes. These types of items can also be organized by category in cloth bins or clear plastic shoe drawers. Of course, you can also store your shoes in these clear drawers, or if you store them in their original boxes, take a picture of each pair and tape it to the outside so you know what's inside.

Pretty much everything else in the closet can be hung up. For pants, I suggest hanging them folded in half on heavy-duty hangers, because lightweight hangers will sag and then snap. Skirts and shorts can go in a short hanging section, while longer dresses and coats will need a full-length hanging space. If hanging space is limited, you can place two pairs of pants on each hanger. You can also buy hangers that have several sets of clips, which allow you to hang multiple shorts or skirts together vertically on one hanger.

If you have the room, I recommend hanging purses side by side. Just slip the straps of one or two bags over the top of each hanger. You can also hang belts by slipping them over the handle of a hanger, or you can purchase a large metal ring designed for belt hanging. For scarves that are smooth and silky, you can drape them over a felt hanger, slightly overlapping one over the next so that a few inches of each scarf are visible. I like to stack thicker scarves on a shelf so it's easy to identify them by looking at the folded edges facing out. As with t-shirts, only stack the piles four or five high at the most to avoid them toppling over. You can also place folded scarves in overlapping layers fanned front to back in a drawer, or in a clear sweater storage bag, which makes it easy to pull the entire pile out and see all your scarves at once.

For jewelry, you can place push pins in a staggered pattern along a wall or on an attractive bulletin board and hang your necklaces and bracelets from them. If you don't have a lot of wall space, you can also carefully hang your necklaces all along the horizontal part of a heavy-duty hanger. You should be able to fit dozens of necklaces on

one hanger, and it's easy to see and remove just one at a time without disturbing the rest.

Maximize your closet's height wherever possible. For example, you can use the space between the floor and the bottom of your skirts or pants for shelving or stacked cubbies for shoes. In the space above your hanging clothes, stack shelves to the ceiling if you can, and get a good step stool for access. These can be used as zone 3 or 4 spots to store things like old tax records, memorabilia boxes, or small suitcases.

—

Maximize your closet's height wherever possible.

—

The clothes closet is a great place to use the zones principle to keep the current season's items front and center. In a smaller space, a good rule of thumb is to place your spring and summer clothes in the closet during the warmer months and containerize your fall and winter items, then switch when autumn arrives. Or, if your closet space is big enough, you can divide the closet in half and use one side for spring and summer and the other side for fall and winter.

I recommend storing off-season clothes in large plastic boxes with lids. Make sure your garments are clean when you store them. Dry clean sweaters and other wooly garments before putting them away and place cedar blocks or lavender and cedar sachets in among

the folded garments. Moths and their larvae, which like to eat dark colors and natural fibers like cashmere and wool, hate the smell of cedar and lavender. (Never use mothballs—these contain nafthalene, which is toxic to humans as well as moths!) Slide the boxes under your bed or store them out of the way on a high closet shelf or down below your in-season items on the floor of the closet. Do not store clothing in cardboard boxes, because over time the boxes can transfer the smell of cardboard and glue onto your clothes, and this smell is very difficult to remove.

In more humid climates, I recommend using drying rods in your closets. These devices are commonly used on boats and work great in closets during the summer. They come with little stands, and when plugged in and placed on the floor, emit a very low heat that will help keep your closet dry and avoid mold growth. Do not store off-season items in attics or basements unless they are sufficiently climate controlled. The fluctuation in temperature and humidity in these spaces can ruin your clothes and shoes.

When deciding what to keep and what to donate as you rotate your clothes each season, use the one-year rule: If you haven't worn it in one year, you probably will never wear it again. (If you love clothes and tend to collect pieces, use a three-year rule instead.) Most people only wear about 20 percent of what's in their closet, so be honest with

WHAT TO TOSS OR DONATE

- ⊘ CLOTHING THAT DOESN'T FIT ANY-MORE OR IS OUT OF STYLE
- ⊘ CLOTHING THAT IS STAINED OR RIPPED BEYOND REPAIR
- ⊘ SHOES THAT HURT YOUR FEET
- ⊘ ANYTHING WITH ELASTIC THAT HAS STRETCHED OUT
- ⊘ ANYTHING YOU HAVEN'T WORN IN ONE YEAR (FOR SPECIAL-OCCASION GARMENTS, KEEP ONLY FOR AS LONG AS THEY LOOK GOOD ON YOU AND ARE STILL IN STYLE)

>> mini TIP: Another great time-saver is to have two laundry bins in your closet to presort your dirty laundry—one for darks and one for lights. This makes it much easier to throw in a quick load of laundry.

yourself as you evaluate each piece. Does it fit? Do you love it? Does it *love* you back? (If you love it, but it doesn't look good on you, it's time to let it go.) I recommend keeping a large shopping bag in your closet so that whenever you notice a garment you haven't worn in over a year or know you will not wear again, you can place it in the bag for donation. Be grateful it was there when you needed it, then pass it to someone else in the world who will be thrilled to have it.

Linen Closets

If you're lucky enough to have a linen closet in your home, it can be utilized in many ways. Of course, you can store your extra linens here. Make sure each set of sheets is complete, then slip the entire set inside one of its coordinating pillowcases. This keeps the closet neater and saves time when making beds since you won't need to rummage through stacks of mismatched sheets. If you've accumulated a lot of sheets over the years, pare down your collection—you should

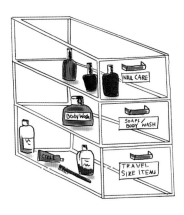

ideally keep only one or two complete sets of sheets for each bed in your home and have one emergency backup mattress pad for each size bed. Stack towels with the folded sides facing out to make it easier to remove the towels one at a time. Keep beach towels all together on one shelf.

The linen closet is also an excellent zone 3 area for spare toiletries and extra supplies, such as paper towels and toilet paper. Keep toilet paper on the floor under the lowest shelf, and store extra soap, shampoo, toothpaste, and other items in clearly labeled bins or stacked clear plastic drawers. You might have categories such as first aid, dental hygiene, nail care, feminine products, and so on—the key is to group items together by category in each container and choose containers that are easy to access. Otherwise, the linen closet is one of those spaces where things can accumulate and get pushed farther and farther back into the dark corners, never to be seen again.

As with the bathroom, this is also another great place to hang a clear plastic shoe bag with plenty of compartments on the inside of the door. You can use this to store extra shampoo, conditioner, hairbrushes, a blow dryer, shaving products, mouthwash, and so on.

If you don't have a linen closet, you can store the sheets for each bed in their corresponding bedroom, perhaps in the closet, under the bed in a plastic storage bin, or in a decorative storage ottoman at the foot of the bed. You can also do this if you're short on clothes closets in your home and then use the linen closet for off-season storage, handbags, or shoes, being sure to maximize the height of each shelf with pull-out drawers or boxes.

Entryway Closets

In your entryway closet, sort each garment by type, category, and season, as well as by person if it's a shared closet. Ideally, keep only the current season's garments in the closet and switch out your spring/summer jackets and fall/winter coats as needed. This is a closet that needs constant maintenance: Every time you rotate the seasonal garments, check to see if they still fit, if you like the style, if they are in good shape, and decide whether anything should be tossed or donated. Clean your off-season coats first, then store them in a climate-controlled area, such as another closet, along with the rest of your off-season clothes. Keep in mind that covering anything in plastic bags will not allow it to breathe, and your garments

can easily develop mold this way. If you can't physically move the out-of-season garments somewhere else for storage, then push them all the way to the side so that the current season's garments are front and center.

For multiple family members, one way to keep everyone organized is to put tabbed name labels on each person's hangers. Of course, this depends on the ages of younger family members. If they can't yet hang up their own clothes, then a coat rack down low outside the closet with a name on each hook is helpful.

The floor beneath the hanging garments is the perfect place to add shelves or cubbies, as pictured below. Keep everything up off the floor and cover any items left on the floor to avoid having dirt and dust bunnies accumulate.

- ⊘ COATS AND JACKETS THAT ARE STAINED, TORN, OR HAVE MOTH HOLES
- ⊘ COATS AND JACKETS YOU HAVEN'T WORN IN ONE TO TWO YEARS
- ⊘ WORN-OUT SHOES THAT ARE BEYOND REPAIR
- ⊘ SHOES YOU HAVEN'T WORN IN ONE TO TWO YEARS
- ⊘ SPORTS EQUIPMENT YOU NO LONGER USE

You can use boxes to collect scarves, gloves, and hats, which should also be grouped by person. A clear shoe bag hung inside the door is a great way to store shoes, gloves, scarves, compact umbrellas, and other small items. Alternatively, you could add several hooks to hang umbrellas, baseball caps, and sun hats. Inside the door is also a good place to hang your pet's leash, harness, or collar.

Sports equipment often ends up in the entryway closet. If that's the case in your house, make sure each group of equipment has its own container, such as one container for all the soccer equipment. You can store these containers on the floor of the closet and easily pull them out so you can clean and vacuum underneath.

If you find that random items show up in this closet, that's your cue to assess what is accumulating, determine what section it goes

into, and decide what zone it belongs in. If, for example, you find bottles of sunblock, towels, and beach bags are thrown in your entry closet in November, it's time to pull

Pro Tip:

If you find you have room for an extra clothing rod in your coat closet, entryway closet, laundry room, or even your pantry, this is an ideal place to hang your tote bags, including beach bags, shopping bags, light travel bags, and overnight bags. Just drape two or three bags on the neck of a sturdy hanger and voilà! You have an organized way to store all your bags so you can easily see and retrieve them.

those out and decide where they go. Check the sunblock and make sure they aren't expired, then put them away in the drawer or box marked for sunblock. Wash the towels and put those away in their designated home, which might be the linen closet or even the laundry room area.

Utility Closets

This closet can take many forms and have a wide range of storage uses in different homes. For example, some homes will have extra space where the HVAC system is, with enough room for you to add some shelving. Others may have a laundry room big enough to add shelves and store items above or around the washer and dryer. In addition to laundry needs, a utility closet can be a great place to store items such as:

- ⊘ Lightbulbs
- ⊘ Tools
- ⊘ Adhesives such as tape and glue
- ⊘ Paper goods
- ⊘ Cleaning supplies
- ⊘ Mop, broom, and dustpan
- ⊘ Vacuum cleaner

When organizing your utility closet, store everything off the floor as much as possible. If there is wall space, you can stagger various hooks or heavy-duty nails on the wall to

PRO TIP:

The ideal set up in a laundry room is to have a flat surface above the washer/dryer with shelving above. If you have stacked or top-loading machines, look for an area nearby large enough to place a small set of folding shelves and use various sizes of containers without lids to store all your smaller laundry items, like stain removers, dryer sheets, dryer balls, mesh lingerie bags, and so on. Make sure the contents of each container are visible. A wall-mounted, flip-down valet hook is ideal for hanging shirts fresh out of the dryer to avoid wrinkles or for air-drying anything you don't want to put in the dryer.

hang the broom, mop, and dustpan, most of which come with either a hook or a hole in the handle perfect for hanging. Depending on the wall and room configuration, you can also use an expandable wall organizer for hanging these items. But if space is a concern, staggering them at various heights will allow you to fit more items and customize how much space you need between each one.

The only items you might need to place on the floor are a bucket with all your cleaning supplies and cleaning cloths, your vacuum, and possibly your toolbox if yours is on the larger side. For everything else, look for a place where you can add shelves to maximize the height of this space. The shelves could be plastic, wood, or vinyl-coated wire.

You can store items like lightbulbs and batteries in a box, if it is clearly labeled in large letters for all family members to see. Clear plastic drawers are another good choice. Ideally, you should have one category of item per box or drawer to avoid a mess. If that's not possible, you can also use drawer dividers to clearly separate each section within the drawer.

Another great storage option for a utility room is a plastic cabinet on wheels. Each drawer can hold one category of items, and clearly labeling each one will help avoid confusion and mixing items. These rolling cabinets typically come in three-drawer or four-drawer sizes. I recommend the four-drawer size if it fits in your utility room. You could have one drawer for lightbulbs, for example, another one for batteries of all sizes, another for your basic tools, and lastly, you could have a drawer for tape and adhesives. (While this may not sound like a broad category, when you think about all

continued on page 68

Expandable wall organizer

TAPE / GLUE

BATTERIES

BASIC TOOLS

LIGHT BULBS

WHAT TO TOSS OR DONATE

- ⊘ CLEANING SUPPLIES YOU HAVEN'T USED IN ONE YEAR OR DON'T LIKE
- ⊘ BROOMS THAT ARE FRAYED OR FILTHY
- ⊘ MOPS THAT APPEAR DIRTY OR SMELL BAD
- ⊘ DETERGENTS THAT ARE OLD AND EXPIRED
- ⊘ CANS AND BOXES OF CLEANERS THAT ARE OLD OR RUSTY
- ⊘ CLEANING CLOTHS THAT ARE TORN OR LOOK DIRTY EVEN AFTER BEING WASHED

MAKING THE MOST OF SHELVING

* If your room has a lot of shelving, add some drawers or bins you can pull out from the shelves to easily access groups of items. You can do this in any room, for anything from office or craft supplies to makeup or baking supplies.

* If the room has a lot of hanging space, there is typically a lot of floor space beneath that and maybe even some unused height between the garments and the floor. This is an ideal place to add inexpensive but highly practical stacking shelves or drawers.

* For a budget-friendly way to make the most of your shelving, you may be able to repurpose found objects, like old gift boxes or baskets, to group items neatly on a shelf. In other cases, you may need to invest in the right storage solutions to fit your shelves — it's worth the investment to stay organized!

NICOLE'S FAVORITES

Mops, brooms, and dustpans hanging on the wall

Valet hook in laundry

Stainless shelves on wheels

the kinds of tape you may have on hand, including packing tape, gray electrical tape, black electrical tape, blue painter's tape, double-sided Scotch tape, and adhesive Velcro fasteners, you can see how they can easily fill a drawer.) The felt dots that go under chairs and tables could also be stored in this drawer. The more commonly used Scotch tape, however, would ideally be stored your zone 1 kitchen or office drawer.

PRO TIPS:

* Always store lighter-weight items higher in the closet and heavier items below.

* Make sure you are using all your vertical space. If there is a large gap at the top or bottom of your clothes closet, for example, add shelves or stacking boxes to take advantage of the height.

* Keep a give-away bag on the floor of your closet and remember to use it frequently.

* Give your closets a regular tune-up: get rid of anything you don't use often or don't need or love anymore. I recommend twice a year; the change of season is a good reminder.

As far as tools go, the utility closet is a good place to store your basics, such as a hammer, a couple of screwdrivers, picture-hanging nails, a level, and a measuring tape, in a drawer. All your other household tools, such as your drill, drill bits, and so on, might be stored in a larger toolbox either here or in the garage.

One last hidden storage opportunity here is the space behind the door. See if a narrow but tall set of shelves with a low front face can be mounted on the wall. Even if it's only four or five inches deep, a set of shallow shelves can be used to store extra canned goods, boxes of pasta, boxes of aluminum foil, plastic bags, extra laundry detergent, and more. This is a great place to keep these extra items accessible but out of the way. You can also place a mounted set of shelves or a clear shoe bag on the back of the door itself to store some of the above mentioned items.

THE OFFICE

An office space presents a unique challenge, which we'll discuss in more detail in Chapter Four on Information Management. But as you think about the types of storage solutions you'll need, keep in mind that the first thing you want to do is get your piles of papers vertical. Horizontal stacking never works. It takes up too much space, and it makes it impossible to see what is in your piles or to access what you need. For help with getting

WHAT TO TOSS OR DONATE

- ⊘ PAPERS AND FILES THAT ARE REDUNDANT OR OUTDATED
- ⊘ EXPIRED INSURANCE POLICIES
- ⊘ SEE CHAPTER FOUR FOR A COMPLETE LIST

things vertical, I recommend bookends as well as file boxes to store things until you're ready to assign them a permanent home. Everyone needs a designated place for their basic desk needs, such as pens, paper, a ruler, scissors, highlighters, and a stapler. It sounds obvious, but a lot of people don't have these things at their fingertips, nor do they have a specific place for them. Part of what creates disorganization is not having what you need right where you need it, when you need it.

THE GARAGE

The garage is an area that many people feel is "out of sight, out of mind." However, it's a great storage opportunity! Plus, the garage is usually the last place you see right before you go out for the day and the first place you see when you get home. If you have a mess of rusty old tools, toys, and equipment thrown all over, that will impact how you feel at the beginning and the end of your day. You want your garage to be neat, organized, and even have pleasing décor on the walls. First and foremost, keep the floor clean. Get almost everything off the floor—yes, that means bikes, chairs, brooms, mops, rakes, toys, your tire pump—everything. The only things I recommend leaving on the floor are large machinery, like a wet vac or lawnmower. Take some time at least once or twice a year to sweep out the garage. This is an area where cobwebs, dust, dirt, sand, leaves, and oils can accumulate, which will only make you want to get out of the garage as quickly as possible! When organized correctly and kept clean, this area has so much potential to help support your organizing projects throughout your home.

—

The garage is usually the last place you see right before you go out for the day and the first place you see when you get home.

—

To maintain order in your garage, add shelving wherever you can along the perimeter. Stainless steel racks on wheels with adjustable-height shelves are ideal. You can also buy heavy-duty plastic shelves from a

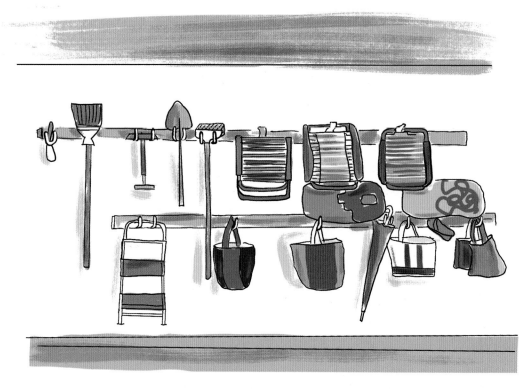

WALL-MOUNTED METAL RACK SYSTEM

home improvement store, but keep in mind that over time, these will bow and not hold up quite as well as metal racks.

Next, buy stackable clear plastic drawers to store similar items in a visible but contained area. These are great for storing anything that does not require climate control, including tools, lightbulbs, and so on. You can also use them to store sports equipment, holiday decorations, and the supplies needed to wash your car, such as cleaning cloths and cleaning products. You might also keep extra tile used in projects in your home, in case you need to do repairs later. Just be sure to clearly label your containers if the contents cannot be easily identified. Do not use cardboard boxes in the garage, as they deteriorate over time and create a buffet for rodents and other critters. Cabinets with doors are another great storage solution for the garage. You can store many of the same items in these, and you get the benefit of doors so you don't have to see everything.

The next thing I recommend in any garage is a metal rack system mounted to the wall that you can use to hang everything from bikes and beach chairs to garden tools and a step ladder. The rack system I love is by Häfele and has a wide variety of hooks and bins available.

Finally, one last item I find so helpful for the garage is large rubber parking bumpers. You're probably thinking, "What? What do I need those for?" Well, they clearly define where your cars go so that you can make use of all available space for storage, add as much shelving and/or cabinetry as you need, and leave adequate walking space.

Remember, the garage is the last thing you see before you leave your house and the first thing you see when you get home. Make it a pleasing place to be, not one you want to run away from!

Tools

There are many options for storing tools. You can keep a smaller, more basic toolbox in a zone 1 or 2 area, such as the pantry, for frequently used items like a hammer, screwdrivers, picture-hanging nails, a tape measure, felt pads for the bottoms of chairs, painter's tape, masking tape, and electrical tape. You can keep the rest of your tools in a master toolbox in another location, such as the garage. The master toolbox should include things like wrenches, a drill, and any other tools that are used less often.

THE BASEMENT

The basement is another great storage option. The key is to have shelves anywhere you plan to store things, to take advantage of the vertical space and keep everything off

WHAT TO TOSS OR DONATE

- ⊘ RUSTY TOOLS, NAILS, HOOKS, AND OTHER HOME REPAIR ITEMS
- ⊘ OLD, DRIED-OUT PAINT
- ⊘ LEAKY OR EXPIRED BATTERIES
- ⊘ EXPIRED CLEANING SUPPLIES
- ⊘ BROKEN OR BENT BEACH CHAIRS
- ⊘ OLD TIRES
- ⊘ BICYCLES THAT ARE BROKEN BEYOND REPAIR
- ⊘ ANYTHING THAT HAS BEEN BROKEN AND LEFT UNREPAIRED FOR MORE THAN TWO YEARS
- ⊘ ANYTHING MOLDY, RUSTY, OR THAT YOU NO LONGER HAVE A USE FOR

the floor. I recommend heavy-duty metal racks on wheels, which you can find online at Amazon or other retailers. These are reasonably priced and easy to assemble and are great for stacking boxes to maximize your space. Without shelving, it's nearly impossible to access stacked boxes without taking apart the whole stack. You can also buy the heavy-duty plastic shelving they have at large home improvement stores, although metal shelves on wheels are a better option. To organize your belongings on the shelves, use see-through plastic bins, or other drawers with a label, so you know what's inside. Store the heaviest items on the bottom and lighter items toward the top.

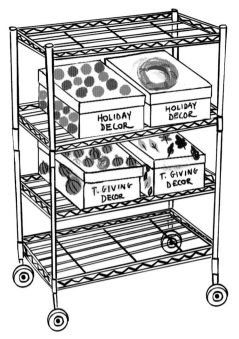

If your basement is not climate-controlled, humidity can be an issue. For a cost-effective solution, you can buy drying rods to help control the humidity level. This will give you the ability to store a greater variety of things. These rods are frequently used on boats to manage the humidity level, and they work well when used in somewhat contained spaces. The alternative is a dehumidifier, which is also a great solution.

Even some furniture can be stored in a climate-controlled basement. But, why are you storing furniture in the first place? If it's for a short period of time, okay. But if you

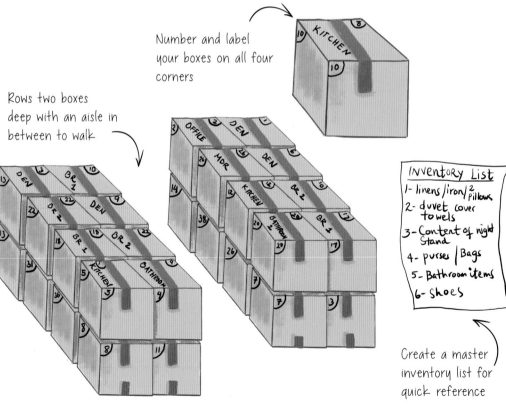

Number and label your boxes on all four corners

Rows two boxes deep with an aisle in between to walk

INVENTORY List
1- linens/iron/ 2 pillows
2- duvet cover towels
3- Content of night stand
4- purses/Bags
5- Bathroom items
6- shoes

Create a master inventory list for quick reference

are storing furniture for posterity, think about whether the next generation is really going to want that old furniture. In my professional experience, 99 percent of the time, furniture that's been stored for years is unwanted and ends up donated or discarded.

—

If your basement is not climate-controlled, humidity can be an issue.

—

Storing memorabilia, photos, and older tax records in a climate-controlled basement is okay, if they are in clearly labeled boxes. You can choose either cardboard or plastic bins with tight-fitting lids. If you are storing clothing, avoid using cardboard boxes and be sure to add cedar blocks or lavender sachets to keep moths away from your clothes. Vacuum-sealed bags are also an efficient and pretty safe way to store your clothes. Only store clothing that is clean and free of dust, debris, or food particles, which can be fertile ground for moths and other bugs. Do a yearly inventory of the clothes you are storing and give away anything you no longer wear.

To make your system more efficient, number the boxes you store in the basement and create a master numerical index list with a brief description next to each number. Keep this list in your filing cabinet or digital filing system (see Chapter Four). Otherwise, it can be very easy to take an out-of-sight, out-of-mind approach to everything that's in your

basement and slowly allow things to accumulate. I recommend rows two boxes wide and four boxes tall with an aisle between each row to prevent just shoving everything into the corners and in piles.

THE ATTIC

To make an attic a practical storage space, first make sure the space is structurally sound enough to withstand the weight of people walking around, as well as the weight of shelving and whatever you plan to store there. The key is to safely add shelving all around the perimeter, and if space allows, create shelving down the center, too. Your shelves can be made of plywood and should be evenly spaced to allow for storing boxes.

Attics can be tricky because they can tend to become a catch-all, and without climate control, it is challenging to keep anything fresh and free of mold and mildew over time. The attic is definitely a zone 4 or 5 location—it's not ideal since it's usually hard

WHAT TO TOSS OR DONATE

- ⊘ SUPPLIES FOR OLD HOBBIES YOU'RE NO LONGER INTERESTED IN
- ⊘ HOLIDAY DÉCOR YOU DON'T USE OR THAT IS DAMAGED OR MISSHAPEN
- ⊘ OLD RECEIPTS AND TAX RECORDS (CHECK WITH YOUR ACCOUNTANT OR LAWYER FIRST)
- ⊘ CLOTHES YOU HAVEN'T WORN IN A YEAR OR MORE
- ⊘ ANYTHING BROKEN, RUSTY, OR MOLDY
- ⊘ ANYTHING YOU KNOW YOU WON'T USE OR HAVEN'T USED IN THREE YEARS OR MORE

to access and is prone to large fluctuations in temperature. Extreme temperature swings can be very hard on clothing and other household items, including furniture.

If your attic reaches very high or very low temperatures, be sure what you're storing can withstand intense heat, cold, and moisture. Never store anything in an attic in a cardboard box, as rodents and other critters are most attracted to natural materials like paper as well as to the glue that holds cardboard boxes together. Instead, opt for large, opaque plastic bins with well-sealed lids.

It's best to store clothes in a cool, dry, and dark area, but if the attic is the only area available, you can store clothing in dark plastic containers with tight-fitting lids to keep out bugs, rodents, and moisture. Vacuum-sealed bags are also okay for attic storage. Avoid storing fine fabrics, photos, candles, shoes, or furniture in the attic. Items that are okay to store in the attic include things like tarps, tents, heavy blankets, gardening tools, extra toilet paper, holiday decorations (such as a faux Christmas tree in a cloth zippered container), and off-season outdoor items, such as an inflatable boat.

—

If your attic reaches very high or very low temperatures, be sure what you're storing can withstand intense heat, cold, and moisture.

—

Make sure you clearly label each box on an outward-facing side. As in the basement, the ideal way to keep track of what you have stored in the attic is to number each box and add it to your inventory list so you can always determine the contents.

Congratulations: you have just completed the three primary principles!

If you have organized your space into sections, created zones based on what you need most, and chosen the right storage solutions for your unique space, you have a strong foundation to build on.

But, just as it takes more than the three primary colors to make a great painting, it takes more than just the three primary principles to stay organized over the long term. In the following chapters, we'll look at three secondary principles that will help you stay organized even on the go and will give you a wide variety of options to achieve a streamlined life that is creative and inspired. Being organized brings serenity, happiness, and success wherever you go!

ACTION STEPS FOR STORAGE SOLUTIONS

1. Within each section, sort your items into zones based on their priority level.
2. Identify the right type of storage (open shelving, boxes, drawers, etc.) for each section.
3. Measure your available storage space and the items you need to store.
4. Search for, buy, and implement your new storage solutions.

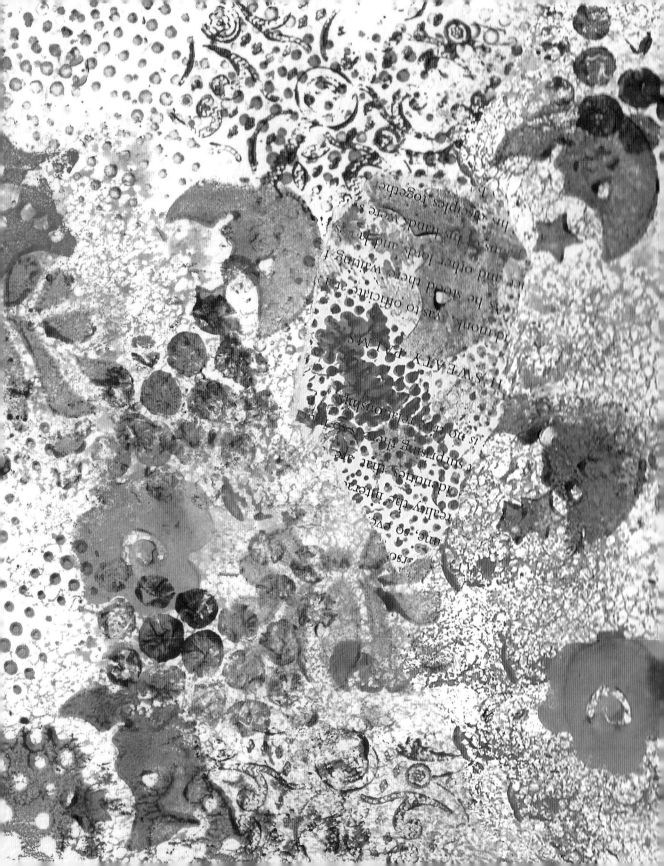

Chapter Four

INFORMATION MANAGEMENT

"Clutter is nothing more than postponed decisions."
—BARBARA HEMPHILL

INFORMATION MANAGEMENT

4

THE FiRST OF THE SECONDARY PRiNCiPLES iN MY ART OF ORGANiZiNG SYSTEM—ORANGE iN OUR COLOR WHEEL—iS

iNFORMATiON MANAGEMENT

The three primary principles we covered in Chapters One through Three provide a basic framework for the art of organizing.

BUT THERE'S MORE TO ORGANIZING than setting up a picture-perfect closet, garage, or desk. Now, let's discuss a few secondary principles of organization that will help you refine your system and stick with it, even when challenges arise. Like the secondary colors that add a layer of depth and complexity to the color wheel, these secondary principles will help fill in the gaps to make your organizational system even more effective, so you can always find exactly what you need when you need it.

The first of the secondary principles is information management. No matter how well-organized your physical space is, you won't feel truly organized without a system to help you manage the flow of information in your day-to-day life. Information management is twofold: there is the outside information coming into your home—mail, bills, calendars, children's school papers, your own work papers, etc.—and then there are the little bits of information—notes, work ideas, decorating ideas, and other miscellanies—that you generate yourself. How do you keep track of and manage this endless flow of information?

I recommend a two-part system: First, create a well-organized filing system. The second component, which will help you keep track of all your little papers, notes, business cards, and ideas, is to create what I call a "halfway book." For more on using the halfway book to stay organized on the go, see Chapter Five.

In a perfect world, all your information would be digital, but as we all know, it's not a perfect world. Even if you prefer to

SUPPLIES CHECKLIST

What You Need for Information Management

- ☑ A FILE DRAWER OR BOX
- ☑ PLENTY OF FILE FOLDERS
- ☑ HANGING FILE FOLDERS WITH INDIVIDUAL PLASTIC TABS
- ☑ STICKY NOTES
- ☑ GARBAGE BAGS/RECYCLING BOX
- ☑ BOXES FOR TEMPORARY FILES
- ☑ PENS
- ☑ SMARTPHONE OR PAPER ADDRESS BOOK
- ☑ INDEX CARDS OR SMALL NOTE-PAD FOR "TO DO" AND "CALL" LISTS, OR THE NOTES APP ON YOUR PHONE
- ☑ LABEL MAKER (MY FAVORITE IS THE BROTHER P-TOUCH™)

manage most of your information from your phone, you'll still need an effective filing system for the papers that inevitably pile up. If you are surrounded by stacks of papers, then you're using what I call the "horizontal" filing system, or, as one of my clients called it, "the clump method." Whatever you call it, this system just doesn't work! When it's in a pile, you can't expect to find anything

quickly or easily. The goal of any successful filing system is to get everything vertical using file folders. Of course, the first step is to sort through all those horizontal stacks so you can determine the best way to group and organize your information.

One of my clients, a high-powered attorney in Manhattan named Colette, is a great example of why information management is so important. Colette had a spacious, gorgeous apartment, but because her stuff was not in order, it never felt big enough. She had never managed to organize her papers at home, so when I first came to her apartment, there were piles of papers in stacks, in boxes, in closets, and in drawers.

When I sit down with a client and see piles of papers everywhere, I know a lot of decisions haven't been made in a while. Every piece of paper is a decision to be made. It's either a to-do, a call, gets filed, or it goes in the trash/recycling. Piles and piles are the paper version of a bottleneck. The main culprit in Colette's case was not having a home for each piece of paper. Because she didn't know where to store the papers, piles accumulated in the most unusual places: under the sofa, in kitchen drawers, even in

>> **mini TIP:** Choose crisp new file folders and use a label maker. The more beautiful your filing system is, the more apt you are to use it!

the bathroom. Once we gathered all the papers, we began the initial sort.

To begin, divide everything into five categories:

⊘ Flats (anything paper that isn't a bill or personal correspondence)

⊘ Bills

⊘ Personal correspondence

⊘ Catalogs

⊘ Magazines

Once everything has been sorted, you can begin to reduce the piles by tossing all the envelopes and other extras that you know you don't need. Then it's time to go through each category of paper, piece by piece.

Colette and I worked in three-hour blocks of time, once a week, for several weeks. We found financial documents, medical insurance policies, old tax returns, plus all sorts of other important papers. During this process, Colette felt a lot of emotions, and there were even

tears—one of her siblings had passed away and she had memorabilia tucked away into other totally unrelated documents. Colette was in the middle of looking through her old bat mitzvah photos when we found her homeowner's insurance policy and the deed to her apartment. In the same boxes with documents, we found Ziploc bags of jewelry and an envelope of cash. We found details on her investments and original stock transaction documents that were important for taxes.

We went through all kinds of policies, important health records, children's report

cards and homework, and more. I separated the children's art into a pile that we could go back to later—some clients choose to photograph the art and create an album so they can discard the art and save space; other times we display the art.

We also found a lot of love letters written between Colette and her husband when they were still dating, and that was also very emotional for her. We made a memorabilia box for each person in the family and another for her sister who had passed away, which

allowed us to move those items away from the filing system. The filing system became very practical and the memorabilia boxes had their own space on a bookshelf.

Pro Tip:

When you begin your initial sort, you may come across items that will trigger your emotions, such as baby toys, photos of your children, old love letters, your own childhood memorabilia, mementos from past jobs or places you've been, and so on. If you know you will be sorting items that could trigger your emotions, you might want to enlist a friend to help. When you find these items, put them in a separate box and set it aside for the time being. To stay focused, you must compartmentalize — you can't bounce back and forth between the emotional process of sorting through your memorabilia and the practical task of creating your filing system. Set aside some time later to organize your memorabilia. Allot two or three hours at a time, at most, to review this box.

When you're ready to store these items, create a separate memorabilia box for each family member. These can be decorative and fit beautifully on a bookshelf. This way, you can enjoy the contents of your box and go down memory lane on a rainy Saturday, as well as use the boxes to store new items as they come up. If a family member's memorabilia start expanding outside their box, you can add another box or get emotionally ready to part with some of the contents. Remember, deciding what to keep is always a matter of balancing what's most important to you with how much space you have.

When you begin the information management process, be sure to start with the current papers that are piling up around your house, many of which may require immediate action. There are other papers that time might have taken care of. If the due date has passed, you know you can toss it. Don't worry about older, already-filed documents just yet—you'll incorporate those into your new, efficient filing system later. Once you've finished your initial sort of the current piles and separated your flats, bills, catalogs, magazines, and personal correspondence, it's time for what I call "touching paper." This means you literally touch every single piece of paper and decide what to do with it.

>> mini TIP: Remember, always file for retrieval, not just to make the piece of paper go away.

For correspondence, you want to quickly assess what the item is and what is being asked of you, then put it on your "to do" or "calls" list or in your calendar immediately (see Chapter Five for more on this). Once you've transferred the important information into your calendar or to-do list, you can toss the paper. For catalogs, try to quickly glance through when they first arrive, or devote an hour to sit down and peruse them all together. Tear out or scan anything you really like, including the website or phone number, and toss the rest of the pages. You can start a file called "things to buy" where you can save all the items you were interested in, in one place. To avoid having magazines pile up, stick with the "current and next" rule, keeping only the current and next months' issues.

When it comes to the flats and bills, again, if there is an immediate task, add it to your to-do list right away. If the paper

Children's artwork photographed and made into a photo book.

I encouraged Colette to answer intuitively, with whatever first came to mind. Sometimes the answer was obvious and important, such as, "That's my homeowner's insurance." I would then ask Colette what label would make the most sense to her for retrieval purposes. Would she prefer to file it under "H" for homeowners, or "I" for insurance? I urge my clients not to worry about getting bogged down with choosing the perfect file name—any name you choose will still be an improvement over no organizational system at all. (It's better to search in two file locations when you need the document than to search through heaps and stacks of paper.)

—

Once you are happy with your file names, you are ready to create labels for your permanent filing system.

Other times, the papers might be less critical, but still important: old notes from classes or lectures, letters from friends, health records, and so on. Again, ask yourself, "Why do I have this, and do I need to keep it?" If so, the next step is to determine how to label it and where to store it. Every piece of paper needs a home. Another thing to ask yourself is, "Does anyone else have a copy of this that I can access, or can I easily find it online?" If so, you can probably shred, recycle, or toss it. (Always check with your accountant or lawyer before getting rid of

is something that needs to be filed, decide whether it should be filed for near-term future reference or for archival purposes. During this initial sort, just separate the papers into broad categories and get rid of anything that is redundant or contains information you can easily find elsewhere. As you touch each piece of paper, ask yourself, "What will I think of when I need this piece of paper in the future?" This detailed process is the first step in developing a filing system.

important financial or legal documents.)

If you decide to keep the paper, the next step is to name it, jot that name down on a sticky note, and place the sticky note on the top edge of your paper so it's sticking up from the top. After you label everything temporarily with sticky notes, use the sticky notes to help you group together all the related items and place them in folders. For example, group together all your papers related to health insurance, old medical records, and so on. (Keep in mind that this is just the first pass, so you'll be naming broad categories. Some of these may eventually need to be broken down further, for example by separating medical insurance records by patient or by a specific medical incident.) Put a sticky note on each folder, give a name to the grouping, then alphabetize the folders.

Finally, review all your sticky notes and make sure they still make sense. Now is the time to re-evaluate any folder names that aren't working and change them, if needed. Once you are happy with your file names, you are ready to create labels for your permanent filing system.

FILING CATEGORIES

Here are some broad-brush categories you may want to use for your files, each of which can be further divided into subcategories:

UTILITIES: Within this category, you can file either by company name or by month. You only need to keep a month or two of your most recent bills, primarily so that you know

>> mini Tip: You don't have a complete system until you place the plastic tabs on the hanging files that will hold your manila folders!

how to contact the company and what your account numbers are, if needed. I recommend also putting the relevant information in your phone or physical address book under the company name.

INSURANCE: Your subcategories might be "car insurance" and "homeowner's insurance." Even if you pay everything online, you should have the original policy document and a declarations page to be filed. And again, the company's phone number, a contact name, and your policy number should be stored in your phone or physical address book, as well as in an easily retrievable file.

MEDICAL: This is a category for which there are typically many subcategories. Each family member needs their own hanging file, and there may be multiple file folders for each family member as well as for each significant medical occurrence.

To complete your system, you'll need a hanging file drawer to store all your newly organized papers. If you don't have a filing cabinet, a plastic file box will work well, if it has side rails for hanging folders. I prefer the type that has a lid with a handle, which makes it easy to transport, if needed. The last step in the process is to place plastic tabs on the hanging file folders that will hold your manila folders. Decide if you are going

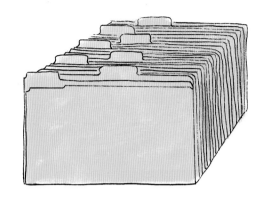

to have your plastic tabs on the right-hand or left-hand side of your drawer, based on how your drawer is oriented. For ease of visibility and flow, keep your plastic tabs all in a row, not scattered throughout your drawer.

Manila folders come in boxes ⅓ cut, which means their tabs for labeling will be at right, left, and in the center. It's helpful to choose either center placement or the opposite side from your plastic tabs—to do this, just flip the ones whose tab placement you want to change inside out! In some

—

The last thing to do is look at any old filing systems you may have and thoughtfully combine them with your new system.

—

cases where a category has subsections, you may have more than one manila folder in a hanging file. In other cases, you may need only one folder per hanging file. While it may seem redundant to label both the file folder tab and the plastic tab, in this case, the hanging file serves as a handy placeholder when you need to remove a manila folder to work on something. When you're ready to return the file to its place, the hanging file tab will remind you exactly where it belongs.

Use heavy-weight manila folders and the tried-and-true regular hanging folders, not the ready-tab style. This might sound boring, or only appropriate for law firms, but I recommend using clear plastic tabs and plain manila folders to make filing and retrieving papers easier. People ask me about color-coded systems. While these sound great, they are harder to maintain, and colored plastic tabs make it harder to read your labels. It's also important to consider how your system looks, and for this reason, I highly recommend using a label maker. This may seem unnecessary, but I find that when files have clean and neat labels, it feels much more uplifting and inspiring to use them. Use white tape with black ink on your label maker. You want to see the label and you want it to be easy to read. There are so many other opportunities to make things fun and whimsical. Don't do it with your files.

The last thing to do is look at any old filing systems you may have and thoughtfully combine them with your new system. Decide if any old file names are still relevant and decide if papers you stored in the past are still needed. (In many cases, you'll find that time has already taken care of it, and you can recycle a lot of these older files.) Then upgrade your old folders to match your beautiful

Pro Tip:

Just like all your other belongings, your files need to be prioritized. Remember the zones concept, which we discussed in Chapter Two, and keep it in mind as you sort your files. For example, older medical files and old tax returns don't need to be in your desk drawer. You might assign those to zone 3 or 4 and place them in a file box to be stored in your basement or attic.

new system. After you have created all your files, it's extra helpful to create an index of every file name in your system for future reference. Simply create a list of all the files in your drawer and print a copy to place at the very front of your file drawer in a file marked "index." I also recommend keeping a digital version somewhere accessible. If you are in a panic dealing with a home or medical emergency, it can be difficult to find the important document you are looking for. An index will help ground you and jog your memory about where you filed a particular document.

Remember Colette, my client with all the papers? Sadly, soon after we completed the organizing system for Colette, there was a fire in her building and her apartment sustained

continued on page 90

WHAT TO KEEP

- Vital records, such as vaccination records, social security cards, adoption papers, birth and death certificates, citizenship papers, marriage certificates, divorce decrees, medical illness records, passports, wills, and letters of last instructions to executors or heirs. If you have a safety deposit box or a safe for your most important paperwork, keep a current list of all your stored documents handy in your file drawer and on your computer.

- Copies of all your tax forms, W-2s, and all relevant documentation, such as charitable receipts and annual dividend payment records, from the past six years plus the current year.

- Bank and financial statements, including sales records of investments, from the past six years, in case of a tax audit.

- Insurance policies: Keep auto, homeowner's, and liability policies for as long as the statute of limitations in the event of late claims. Keep disability, medical, life, personal property, and umbrella policies for as long as you own the policy or are a beneficiary of that policy.

- Car records, such as title or lease agreement.

- Home improvement records and receipts.

- Home purchase and inspection documents.

- Major home appliance receipts, warranties, and instruction manuals.

- Mortgage documents.

- Investment purchase records.

- Medical records: Keep those that pertain to chronic or ongoing conditions or to significant incidents or findings, like major surgery. If you're dealing with an ongoing medical issue, you may want to get a large three-ring binder to store all relevant information in tabbed sections. If you have regular blood work, create a "blood work" file to make it easy to view your history and trends. Though your doctor will keep records, it's only for a limited time and it's good to have all the pertinent data at your fingertips in case you need a second opinion or want to change doctors.

WHAT TO TOSS, SHRED, OR RECYCLE

- Toss pay stubs after checking them against your W-2 forms.

- For magazines, a good rule of thumb is to keep only the current and next month's issues All previous months get recycled. Also, when you come across a favorite article you want to keep, just keep the article and toss the source!

- Toss credit card statements after a year and receipts after you have checked them against the card statements (unless you need them to show proof of purchase or payment, or for tax reasons). The exception is receipts from recently purchased items that you might want to return. Keep these in a file labeled "current receipts" for no more than a year. If you are a sole proprietor, set up files representing the deductible categories of your business and file your receipts daily or weekly.

- Toss old medical insurance paperwork as soon as the claims have been reviewed and settled and bills have been paid. If you need to refer to this info later, it's available on your insurance company's website for a limited time. You can also make digital scans of medical paperwork as needed and file those away for retrieval. Make sure you know why you're keeping these now-settled documents—for example, if it's because there are contact names and numbers, you may want to file those directly into your phone book.

- Toss bills as soon as they have been paid. Your digital check images or credit card statements are your proof of payment, so there's no need to keep the paper bills.

a lot of fire damage. Luckily, all she had to do was pull out her homeowner's insurance file, which she easily found in her new file drawer, and she knew who to call, what her policy number was, and everything else she needed. Colette called to tell me how grateful she was for her organized system and that we had taken the time to do it.

USING YOUR NEW SYSTEM

Now, you have a beautiful, well-functioning file system. So, how do you keep it that way?

It's all about flow. For you to have a clear desk, new incoming papers must be filed into their home regularly. They won't jump into the files by themselves!

Every night, take a moment to file any new papers that have come in. Try setting a timer and aim to return everything to its place in fifteen minutes. If you don't let your papers pile up, this should only take a few minutes. The result is that you stay in control of your information and can retrieve anything at a moment's notice. If you're not able to devote fifteen minutes each day, be prepared to spend a couple of hours every Saturday filing. If you don't maintain your system regularly, it will quickly fall apart, and you may need to call in a professional to get back on track.

As you spend time sorting and filing, throw away what you no longer need. How do you know what to keep and for how long? Always check with your accountant or lawyer before throwing away any financial or legal papers. If you take the time to maintain your system regularly, you will be able to enjoy a functional, uncluttered workspace and a clear mind. In the next chapter, Portability, we will discuss how you can take this system on the road with you. In today's world, it's more important than ever to be flexible and have a system that is portable, so you can pivot quickly to meet all the ever-changing demands on your time.

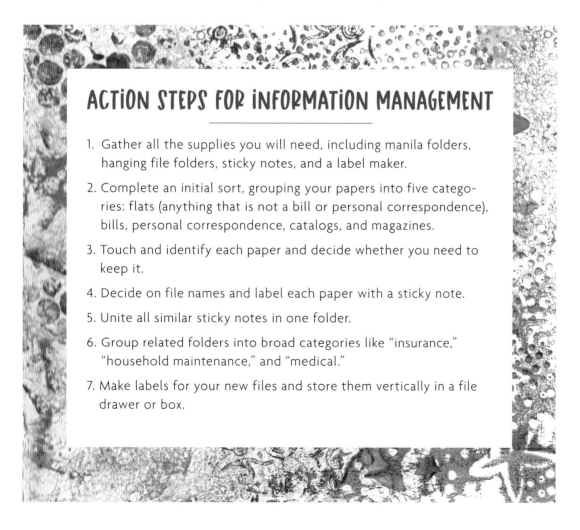

ACTION STEPS FOR INFORMATION MANAGEMENT

1. Gather all the supplies you will need, including manila folders, hanging file folders, sticky notes, and a label maker.

2. Complete an initial sort, grouping your papers into five categories: flats (anything that is not a bill or personal correspondence), bills, personal correspondence, catalogs, and magazines.

3. Touch and identify each paper and decide whether you need to keep it.

4. Decide on file names and label each paper with a sticky note.

5. Unite all similar sticky notes in one folder.

6. Group related folders into broad categories like "insurance," "household maintenance," and "medical."

7. Make labels for your new files and store them vertically in a file drawer or box.

BEHIND THE SCENES

When I started my career at 22 years old, I had big dreams.

I had studied textile design and fashion in college, but after taking an elective class in TV production, I was hooked and decided I wanted to work in production at MTV more than anything in the world. Through plenty of perseverance, I won a job as an assistant in MTV's international department. It was my dream job. I knew little about working in a corporate environment and had only a rudimentary knowledge of TV production, but I was excited about the opportunity and willing to work hard.

At first, I was overwhelmed. I didn't know how to control the chaos of the busy production department. Once I learned to use a daily planner and a halfway book,

I was able to manage my calendar as well as my boss's calendars. Next, I had to address the mountains of paper on my desk. It had become so disorganized that every time I took out a pen to write something down, I would lose the pen somewhere in the piles. It was maddening. I knew I had to come up with a solution fast—thus began my love affair with file folders. I had a few of them in different colors, but I was afraid to use too many because they were expensive. I quickly realized, though, that if I wanted to keep my job, I needed to order more file folders, use them liberally and label them carefully. This was the genesis of my information management system.

I created a system that was intuitive to me since I was the one who would primarily be using it. I used broad categories and then subcategories, eventually assigning a whole drawer to one or two subjects. I reported to three high-powered executives, so I gave each boss their own drawer.

As I began to clear my desk, more and more assignments came my way. First, I was assigned the task of answering fan mail for Daisy Fuentes, the VJ on our show at the time. They handed me boxes and boxes of unanswered mail. I created a system to organize it and answered every single letter (even the strange ones sent from prisoners). Then I was tasked with creating what was known as a "music cue sheet" to credit the artists of each video played on our show, "MTV Internacional," a half-hour weekly show in Spanish. On each episode, we played approximately six videos, and I went through hundreds of songs and created a system to issue a credit to each

artist. I discovered that I enjoyed these highly detailed assignments, and all the while I was gaining knowledge in creating and maintaining systems.

One of my bosses began working on MTV Asia, a new network launching in Hong Kong. She would travel to Hong Kong and sometimes stay for a month or more at a time. She was also the director for the other MTVs around the world, which at the time included MTV Brazil, MTV Europe, MTV Japan, and MTV Australia. With so much paper and information coming across my desk, I needed a system to smoothly transition the appropriate information to my boss in Hong Kong and file the rest. These early days at MTV were an on-the-ground crash course in information management and planted the seeds for the systems I still use to manage my time and information today.

Chapter Five

PORTABILITY

"Organizing isn't about perfection, it's about efficiency, reducing stress & clutter, saving time & money, and improving your overall quality of life."

—CHRISTINA SCALISE

PORTABILITY

THE SECOND OF THE SECONDARY PRINCIPLES IN MY ART OF ORGANIZING SYSTEM—GREEN IN OUR COLOR WHEEL—IS

PORTABILITY

In Chapter Four, we learned how to manage the flow of paperwork in and out of a space and develop a neat, organized filing system for information management.

BUT A TRULY FUNCTIONAL SYSTEM can't stop at your file drawer—it needs to successfully address how you spend your time and be flexible and portable enough to go with you out into the world as you move from one place to another. This brings us to the fifth principle of organization, the principle of portability.

Portability describes a system that will keep you organized at home, in the office, and on the road. If you tend to collect little papers throughout the day—business cards, notes you jotted down in a meeting, that phone number someone gave you for the plumber—I have a solution for your "little paper syndrome."

With the portability system, outlined in this chapter, you

can be busy all day at work, running errands, carpooling, attending meetings, and more, and still have everything you need at your fingertips to keep track of appointments, notes, and other information.

In my experience, creating a portable information management system was an evolution. When I began my corporate career in 1990 at MTV, the office was like controlled chaos, and it wasn't long before my desk was covered in mountains of papers and envelopes. This was back in the day of interoffice envelopes, and everything came across my desk for all the people in my department. One of my bosses noticed I was buried in papers and was having trouble keeping up and suggested I take a course on the Franklin Planning System. It was a life-changer for me. The Franklin Planning System taught a way to prioritize your daily tasks in a planner and keep track of how you spend your time on spacious pages. Appointments were arranged vertically on one page, with the facing page available for notes and to-do lists. According to the system, each year's planner was kept for five years for future reference.

Eventually I wanted a smaller version of my daily planner, which I continue to use to this day. I use the Filofax brand, but any planner works. I learned that your planner only needs to hold two or three months at a time, and the rest of the pages can be stored in your desk. It's important to choose a planner with a "month-at-a-glance" calendar because by flipping back and forth between the day on a page and the whole-month view, you can easily plan your days, weeks, and months.

My boss at MTV also gave me a spiral notebook

MARCH 2015
THRU
OCT 2015

and model. Like many actors, I needed a part-time gig to pay the bills. When a friend asked me to help her organize her office, I came up with the idea of starting an organizing business. In my new freelance life, I bounced between working in a client's home or office, auditioning, taking classes, booking jobs, and performing. I began accumulating lots of little papers and seemingly random notes, and it was difficult to keep track of everything. Realizing that I needed a better way to manage all the information coming at me in a categorical manner, I remembered the

—

I called it my "halfway book" because it is exactly that—a place to gather the information that was halfway between very important and random bits of information that I might never need.

—

and taught me the virtues of writing everything down. I kept a sort of running tally collection of notes in the notebook, which would later evolve into my "halfway book" (more on this later). These two new tools, the planner and the notebook, helped me to realistically quantify the amount of time I allocated to each task so I could manage my time more effectively and be more productive.

As I continued in my TV production career, I learned the importance of creating an up-to-date to-do list at the end of each business day. My to-do list became the blueprint for the next day and creating it at the end of the day meant I was ready to get to work as soon as I came into the office in the morning. This is a habit I continue today.

Eventually, I moved from the production side of things to begin working as an actress

spiral notebook my boss had given me at the beginning of my career. Using that notebook as inspiration, I created a system to keep everything portable and organized.

I called it my "halfway book" because it is exactly that—a place to gather the information that was halfway between very important information and random bits of information that I might never need. Sometimes, those little notes jotted down on the fly would prove to be important enough to go into a more permanent file or notebook; in other cases, I didn't need them again. Since you don't always know at first, having a designated holding place to store these bits of information in a retrievable, organized way can be enormously helpful. I still use this system religiously!

For my halfway book, I use a notebook with twelve precut tabbed sections. The tabs allow me to keep track of different categories of information in an easily retrievable manner. I date each book, and one notebook typically lasts me about six months. Of course, everyone is different, so you may go through a halfway book more or less quickly

depending on the volume of information you collect in your daily life. I once worked with a famous cinematographer who remarked that in his job, he would fill one notebook every day! So, for him, we adapted the system to fit

SUPPLIES CHECKLIST
What You Need for Portability

- ⊘ A PHYSICAL DATEBOOK OR A CALENDAR PLANNING APP
- ⊘ A NOTEBOOK, BINDER, OR NOTE-RETRIEVAL APP FOR YOUR "HALFWAY BOOK".
- ⊘ A LABEL MAKER (I LIKE THE BROTHER P-TOUCH)
- ⊘ YOUR SMARTPHONE
- ⊘ A COMMITMENT TO YOUR CHOSEN METHOD!

Halfway book interior

in a large three-ring binder with divider tabs and removable pages. Whatever type of book you use, the key is to have designated tabs for each category of information that you tend to collect on a regular basis.

Once I had my planner and halfway book set up, I was ready to rock and roll. As I ran from a morning organizing client on the Upper East Side, to an audition downtown, to a meeting with an agent, and so on, my planner kept me on schedule, my halfway book kept track of all the needed information such as addresses and client notes, and my to-do list, updated nightly, helped me start each day on the right foot.

I have since taught this system to hundreds of people, both one-on-one and in workshops, seminars, and classes, and people call me often to tell me how much it has helped them. It's easy to take it on the road with you wherever you happen to be, and it works for any lifestyle, from a mom waiting in the carpool line, to a general contractor working on a busy construction site, to a lawyer, businessperson, or student. It's adaptable and can work well in digital format, too.

Now, let's look at how you can apply the portability system to organize your business and personal life.

THE HALFWAY BOOK

The first item to have at your fingertips is a catchall notebook with tabbed sections. You can choose a spiral-bound notebook or a three-ring binder. (The book I used for nearly two decades was a 6¾-x-8⅝-inch Clairefontaine notebook with twelve tabs and sixty sheets). Create as many tabs as you need for the categories that are relevant to you. (I use my label maker on the smallest font for this.) For example, you might have one tab for each member of

Pro Tip:

Maximize your A-Z. Store lists of information for easy retrieval. You can do this in the contacts section of your smartphone or the A-Z section of your paper planner, or use your phone's Notes app or a list app like Anylist to create an alphabetized list of categories that will make your notes easily retrievable. Use these resources to keep ongoing lists of things like:

- ⊘ Babysitters
- ⊘ Books to read
- ⊘ Dog walkers
- ⊘ Movies to watch
- ⊘ Restaurants you like
- ⊘ Restaurants you want to try
- ⊘ Websites to check out

your household and one or more tabs for your work life. Perhaps you'll designate one for a special project you are working on, such as a renovation, decorating project, or plans for an upcoming trip. You might want a health and medical section to keep track of health tips and doctor recommendations. Everyone's categories will be different, but the key is to make sure your halfway book includes space for each category of information that regularly comes your way.

———

The idea is to provide a home for all the notes and papers you accumulate daily with an easy retrieval method.

———

The idea is to provide a home for all the notes and papers you accumulate daily with an easy retrieval method. If you receive information in the form of a handwritten note or other written reminder, you can tape it right into the book. Creating customized categories will help you easily refer to and retrieve infor-

mation—much more efficient than flipping through pages and pages of random notes. The halfway book is important as a holding place for the tidbits of information that may eventually go into your permanent files or may simply remain in the book. It's important to date each notebook in the front—for example, from January to April of the current year—and hang onto these notebooks for approximately five years in case you need them.

These days, of course, many people prefer a digital system to manage their time and information. Whatever its format, a successful system needs to offer a way to organize all those random bits of paper that seem to land on desks or get bunched in purses or pockets or wallets. If you prefer to store your information digitally, you can scan all those little sticky notes and handwritten reminders and save them in a categorized virtual retrieval system. I recently began using an app called Rocketbook. With Rocketbook, you write your notes on special paper and scan them into the app, then erase the page

>> mini TIP: When creating your daily schedule, remember to allow time for all your activities, including meetings, appointments, errands, your kids' activities and carpools, exercise, personal time, and so on. Then add in some extra buffer time because tasks often take longer than we think.

SHOULD I CHOOSE A PAPER OR DIGITAL PLANNER?

It really depends on the way you think. Don't try to be a square peg in a round hole! There's no one right way to get organized; the method you should choose is the one that works best for you. Here are some tips to help you decide.

CHOOSE A PAPER PLANNER IF:

Your thinking flows most easily when you're writing things out, pen on paper.

You tend to remember where on a page you wrote something down. (e.g., "I wrote the phone number on the right-hand corner of the page in red pen.")

You like to flip back and forth to view your schedule on paper from both a daily and monthly perspective.

You write your to-dos in categories (e.g., things to buy, work tasks, errands, calls) rather than in terms of sequence, priority, or chronology.

You find physical, tactile reminders help keep you on track.

CHOOSE A DIGITAL PLANNER IF:

Your thinking flows easily from fingers to keyboard.

You generally remember appointments by the date, the day of the week, and the time of day. (e.g., "The concert is on a Tuesday, two days after my husband's birthday on Sunday the 26th.")

You can look at a screen representing a part of a day or week and visualize the whole.

You write your to-dos in terms of sequence, priority, and chronology rather than by category.

You like to use your phone's search function to find the calendar or contact information you need.

You prefer to streamline what you take with you each day or tend to lose track of your belongings.

You might decide to use a combination of paper and digital. Either way, an effective information management system is one that allows you to easily store and retrieve all the information you need daily.

with a damp cloth so you can reuse it to add more information and images. It's amazing. The scans are picture-perfect and if I write the category word at the top of the page surrounded by hashtags (e.g., "##Health and Medical##"), the app will automatically name the page so I can file it in a retrievable folder in any cloud-based software I choose.

THE DAILY PLANNER

To complement your halfway book, you need a datebook to serve as your go-to place for all appointment information. This very important item can be either digital or paper. For a paper system, Filofax, the Franklin Planner, the Hobonichi system and the Bullet Journal are popular choices, and each one is every bit as efficient as the next. If you prefer a digital system, Cozi is a great planning app for the whole family. You can also try Google Calendar or search the app store to find your favorite. Pick a format that works for you and stick with it.

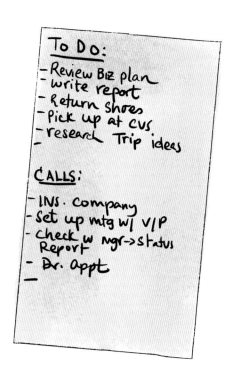

TO DO:
- Review Biz plan
- write report
- Return shoes
- Pick up at CVS
- research Trip ideas
-

CALLS:
- INS. company
- Set up mtg w/ VIP
- check w/ mgr→status Report
- Dr. appt
-

>> **Digital Tip:** If you prefer a digital system, check out the app store for productivity apps like Evernote, Onenote, or Trello. But remember that a categorical retrieval method is important to help you tame those piles of little papers. Even if you're just using the most basic notes app, creating category titles to help you retrieve information is key.

Kids' Tip:

Place all your children's schedules in clear plastic sleeves and keep them together with a metal ring. Hang these in a visible place, like the kitchen, so everyone in the family knows where to find them. Remember to jot down all pickup and drop-off times in your planner to keep yourself on track!

Your planner should work together with the halfway book: when you set a new appointment, use the planner to note the time of the appointment and use the halfway book for all related notes. If you're working with a paper system, I suggest using the day-on-a-page layout to note appointments in the right time slot and referring to this page throughout the day. In addition, you can use the month-at-a-glance layout, which shows the whole month at once across two pages. On this page, mark your appointments clearly, simply, and briefly, so you can see immediately how best to manage your time within the

—

Whenever you leave the house,
remember to take your halfway book
and planner with you, just as
you make sure you have your cell
phone and keys.

—

context of the whole month. For example, if you want to plan something for three weeks from now, it's easier to look at the entire month at once in order to schedule a time.

If you are using a digital system, you can easily maintain it as you regularly input new entries. When quick input isn't possible, tuck the information away in your halfway book until you have more time for updating.

When choosing a planner, it is important to include a phone and address book to keep this information portable. Whether you prefer paper or digital, plan to do regular data entry. Your planner will be like your personal bible—your datebook for all appointments, including personal time, along with all the important phone numbers and addresses you need. Always keep it with you.

Whenever you leave the house, remember to take your halfway book and planner with you, just as you make sure you have your cell

Pro Tip:

Keeping a current to-do list for your daily, weekly, and monthly tasks is another essential part of a successful portability strategy. This list should be separate from your planner and your halfway book, because your to-do list will constantly change, and when you're done with a task, you're done! You can use a classic index card to keep track of daily tasks or create a list on your phone or computer. Either way, the key to staying organized is updating your list every night. I recommend starting on Sunday night by taking some time to plan out your week. It can also be helpful to keep an ongoing call list and a things-to-buy list. Frequently check your lists to stay on track. You'll be efficiently breezing through life before you know it!

phone and keys. If you decide not to carry the halfway book with you every day, be sure to have it on your desk waiting for you at the end of the day. Whenever you start accumulating little papers, you'll know it is time to transfer the information to your halfway book.

A few years ago, I worked with a client named Amy who ran a busy household with three school-aged kids. When I first came to her house, she showed me the lovely flip-style wall calendar she was using, with 1½-inch square boxes for each day of the week. She told me that she was having a lot of trouble keeping track of everyone's schedules, including pickups, drop-offs, events, due dates for school assignments, etc. The first thing I suggested was that she needed more room to write everything down. There was simply no way all that scheduling and planning could be done in a 1½-inch square space. I showed her how to use a planner with a full page for each day, as well as a halfway book. As soon as she had more space to keep track of everyone's information, the planning for her family of five immediately began to run more smoothly.

Whatever your lifestyle—whether you work behind a desk, are an entrepreneur or freelancer, are a busy parent, or all of the above—one thing is certain: A reliable system is essential to keep it all together.

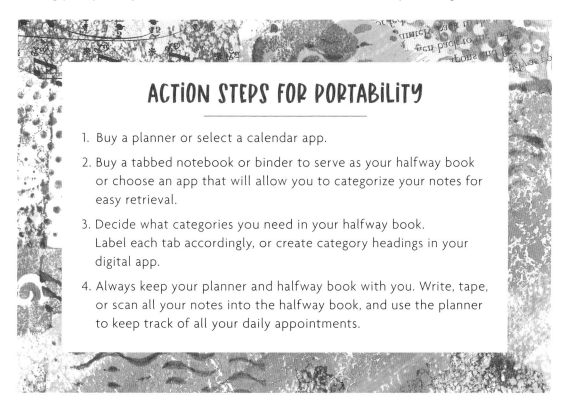

ACTION STEPS FOR PORTABILITY

1. Buy a planner or select a calendar app.
2. Buy a tabbed notebook or binder to serve as your halfway book or choose an app that will allow you to categorize your notes for easy retrieval.
3. Decide what categories you need in your halfway book. Label each tab accordingly, or create category headings in your digital app.
4. Always keep your planner and halfway book with you. Write, tape, or scan all your notes into the halfway book, and use the planner to keep track of all your daily appointments.

Chapter Six

BACK TO ONE

Bringing it all together.

Time is a created thing. To say "I don't have time" is to say "I don't want to." —LAO TZU

THE THIRD OF THE SECONDARY PRINCIPLES IN MY ART OF ORGANIZING SYSTEM—PURPLE IN OUR COLOR WHEEL—IS

BACK TO ONE

Remember Steve from Chapter One? Well, we finally managed to assign a place for everything in his house and label things in a way that was intuitive for him.

STEVE KNEW WHERE TO FIND his aspirin, sunglasses, and any paper or file for work, and could return any object to where it belonged with ease. Once he was able to stay organized, he felt more productive and was having more fun in all areas of his life. He felt comfortable inviting guests over and his home felt like a relaxing place. When his children visited, they were able to play and then put their things away because every storage container was labeled and in place.

As Steve's story shows, an organizational system that works well can be truly life changing. But getting things sorted and put away is only the first step. To truly change your life, an effective system must not only be flexible enough to grow and adapt with you but also easy enough for you to maintain, day after day and year after year.

When I was working in TV production early in my career, one thing I heard over and over while shooting was "**back to one**!" This basically meant, "Everyone get back to your original starting point, where you were when we began shooting." A lot of work goes into creating a TV production set, from the props to the furniture placement to the carefully calibrated lighting. Once the director yells "action!" and the scene begins shooting, everything gets moved around, so the set may look

Pro Tip:

You must have a maintenance schedule for getting "back to one!"

Schedule a little clean-up time—about 15 minutes—at the end of each day and make it part of your routine.

You'll also need periodic tune-ups of your overall system to keep up with your changing life—usually once a year is enough.

quite different by the time the director calls "cut." If another take is needed, the director will say, "Okay, everyone, **back to one**!" and everything is placed back exactly as it had been, ready to shoot again from the original starting place.

Your home organization, just like a TV production set, needs to have a **back to one** to be a truly sustainable, effective system—and you need to be able to get to that place quickly and easily on a daily basis. Like the lighting, set, and prop designers who carefully create a stage set, you must first determine your baseline and establish what your space should look like when everything is put away in its assigned home. Of course, as you live and work in that space, things will get moved around, but if you know where **back to one** is and how to get back there, you'll easily maintain your clean, well-organized space.

—

Your home organization, just like a TV production set, needs to have a "back to one" to be a truly sustainable, effective system.

—

I recommend you spend at least ten to fifteen minutes at the end of each day to work on getting **back to one**. This is a key factor in staying organized—papers won't fly into the files by themselves, your clothes won't jump onto their hangers, and the dishes on the counter won't stack themselves neatly in the cabinets. Taking a few minutes per day to return things to their proper homes is an easy job, but if you don't take the time to do it daily, you'll find you need to devote two or three hours on the weekend to get things **back to one**. However you achieve it, I recommend that everyone get **back to one** by each Sunday night. The last thing anyone wants is to wake up on Monday morning already feeling discombobulated because their house or office is a mess. When the week begins, you want to start off feeling at the top of your game.

Organizing is a discipline, just like starting a diet or practicing yoga: you don't stop the day you reach your goal; you must stick with your new habits to continue moving in a positive direction. Maintaining your new system is essential to your well-being and self-care.

• • •

Another client of mine, Margarete, a Manhattan resident who lived in Beekman Place, had a palatial apartment that was impeccable.

As she walked me through her home, which was in perfect order, I wondered why she had hired me. Then she showed me the room where her two young daughters, ages three and five, slept. Their room was a total wreck: there were dolls and doll clothes; markers, crayons, coloring books, and drawing paper; stuffed animals; clothing and hair accessories; and play kitchen items like fake hamburgers and plastic drinking glasses, everywhere. "I just can't get them to pick up or put things away!" Margarete said.

The problem, of course, was that her daughters didn't know where to put things. They didn't have a clear *back to one*. The girls couldn't read yet, so we bought clear plastic drawers and sorted all the different items into them. We then put a picture on each box, so they could clearly see where the dolls would go, where the coloring books would go, where the markers and crayons would go, and so on. Margarete had a chest for their clothes, but everything was just thrown in, so we rearranged the closet, too, and made sure the kids knew where everything went. Kids will be kids, but once we established a *back to one*, it was easier for them to return their clothes and toys to their proper places. So, at the end of each day, in just a few minutes and with a little help from mom, they could put everything back in order.

Once you have your *back to one*, it's generally easy to maintain it by getting rid of excess and putting everything back where it belongs. To maintain this flow, pay attention to your surroundings and over time you will develop an internal gauge that keeps you on track.

If a drawer starts overflowing, a table becomes overrun with papers, or a closet is suddenly too crowded for you to find things easily, that is a sign that it's time to reassess that spot. If you must force it, stuff it, or

---

If you must force it, stuff it, or hide it, that's your trigger to deal with the bottleneck and get that space back to one.

---

hide it, that's your trigger to deal with the bottleneck and get that space *back to one*. Often, a bottleneck occurs because you've bought too much, or because you stopped that daily practice of getting completely *back to one*. When this happens, you need to get rid of excess and keep only the most important and useful objects in every zone 1. If your t-shirt drawer is overflowing, that's a sign that it's time to get rid of your older, less frequently worn t-shirts. If your kitchen utility drawer is jammed full, there are probably things in there that don't belong in zone 1. Take out any zone 2 or zone 3 items and move them into clear drawers to store in the linen closet or under the kitchen sink.

A question many of my clients ask when dealing with a bottleneck like this is, "What if

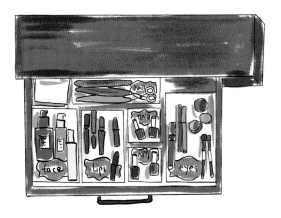

I can't get to this right now?" The temptation is to grab a box or a bag, drop all your extra stuff into it, and set it aside somewhere. Don't do it. Corral a whole lot of stuff if you must, but don't make it so comfortable that you can ignore it. That's the key. Instead, put it in a pile on your desk where it will be in your way. That way you'll be forced to address it sooner rather than later. Always whittle away at your bottleneck collection by getting rid of the obvious first, then putting everything else into its proper zones daily.

Even better, try to avoid creating bottlenecks in your space at all, by establishing what I call an "in-and-out flow." I have a personal rule: if I buy three new tops and two pairs of shoes, I immediately get rid of three items of clothing and two pairs of shoes. This in-and-out flow keeps my system functioning well, and it can be applied to every section of your home, from your purse to your kitchen drawer to your kids' toy box. If you bring something new into your home, get rid of something that is older or made redundant by the new item. It's important that you love everything you own and you don't get bogged down with extra items.

This can be challenging when it comes to categories of things that you really enjoy. For example, I love makeup, so I tend to accumulate it. But I don't need sixteen eyeshadows or ten lipsticks, so I make it a point to regularly go through my collection and get rid of anything old and anything that I don't use often.

There's no need to fear letting go of four shirts in your closet when you just bought four more. You have enough. If you have established a solid **back to one**, then you can have faith that you already have enough and there is no need to accumulate more. The more excess you have, the more difficult it is to get **back to one**. If you find that there truly are missing elements in your space, make a list and commit to buying only those items.

This approach will not only keep your space organized, but will also save you money. When you know you need to manage your in-and-out flow, you won't be as tempted to buy a pair of shoes just because

---

If you bring something new into your home, get rid of something that is older or made redundant by the new item.

---

they are $65 on sale instead of $300. If you wouldn't buy them if they weren't on sale, you probably don't really love the shoes themselves; you just love that you're getting a deal. But that deal will cost you over the long term because you will accumulate things you don't love and clutter up your closet. Don't get seduced by a sale rack.

As you shop and organize, always ask yourself, what do I really need to be happy?

If getting rid of sentimental items is hard for you, you can take a picture of each item before you place it in a bag to be donated.

How much do I need to be happy? After all, isn't that the point? How many shoes can you really wear? The answer is different for everyone—for some people, it might be fifty pairs, because they want to wear something different every day. But most people only wear 10 to 20 percent of what's in their closet. You should only own what you can store comfortably and actually wear.

My own clothing closet is pretty maxed out. I have other closets in the house I could start shoving stuff into, but I never do that. I like to leave extra room to grow and change. Besides, if I can't see my clothing, I won't wear it! Always leave some empty space in your home to allow for physical expansiveness and room to think, be creative, and make space for your emotions.

Items with sentimental value can often present a challenge but it's important to be honest with yourself. When you inherit something that belonged to a parent or a friend, ask yourself if you really love it. If not, deal with it before it balloons into a disaster. I often hear clients say things like, "I bought those boots in Italy thirty years ago and they were so expensive! I can't possibly get rid of them! But I haven't worn them in twenty years." I always think, "Well, someone else could use these and would love to have them." Remember that your memories don't live inside any physical item—you can let the boots go and still keep your memories of that Italy trip. If getting rid of sentimental items is hard for you, you can take a picture of each item before you place it in a bag to be donated. If you haven't gone looking for something in twenty years, you likely won't miss it when it's gone, and there is always someone out there in the world who needs that item more than you and will enjoy it tremendously.

If you find that you're accumulating piles or a mess and you know you haven't brought ten new items into your home, that's a sign that there are items that need to be put away. Always think of how to keep things flowing. If you need to donate stuff, donate it right away, before it can create a bottleneck. If you need to mail letters, send them when you have three, don't wait for fifteen to pile up. Take the time to regularly get rid of what you don't need, so that you never allow the bottleneck to overrun your home—this is the flow that will help you get **back to one** each day and week. Establish some personal rules, make a commitment to yourself, and you will maintain your system over the long term.

I used to get something I called "the Sunday blues," where I would be a little sad that the weekend was ending and that I'd have to start the weekday grind over again on Monday morning. After I developed the six basic principles of *The Art of Organizing*, my Sundays didn't feel so depressing. I had a sense of purpose because, by Sunday night, I knew I had to get everything **back to one** and make myself a to-do list and a call list. It felt great to start my week with a plan and with everything in its place. If you want to remain the master of your own space, you can't ignore all the stuff that piles up and walk over it or around it. Keeping your space neat is like brushing your teeth—there are no shortcuts, and if you skip it, you will get

cavities. Staying organized is the same way; maintenance is key. And it's about much more than just having a neat-looking space: it's about self-care and quality of life.

When I was going through the water-damage issue I will share with you on p. 116, I suddenly understood many of the feelings my clients have shared with me over the years in a whole new way. Looking

—

Establish some personal rules, make a commitment to yourself, and you will maintain your system over the long term.

—

at the jumbled pile drying out on my basement floor, I felt frustrated, embarrassed, depressed, and angry. I swung back and forth between wanting to close the door and run away from it, to feeling helpless, to pretending that it just didn't matter—but deep down I knew it did matter to me. The clutter started taking up space in my mind, and when I tried to go to sleep at night, I would ruminate over the various ways I could tackle this huge pile.

When I first decided to call in my colleague to help, my friends thought I was joking. How could an organizer need an organizer? Well, at some point or another we all need a little help, and it's okay to ask for it. After my colleague Julie helped me get back on track, I felt a huge sense of relief. It

—

To be organized is to be successful, and you, too, can have a beautiful and organized life.

—

was the most incredible feeling to have it all sorted. Now, every time I go to that part of the basement, I am so happy to know where things are—and I am sleeping well at night!

I hope the principles in this book will help you organize your life in a way that makes sense to you and is sustainable for your lifestyle. Armed with the six *Art of Organizing* principles, you can create a truly organized home and a happier, healthier, more streamlined existence. Like an artist using all the colors on the color wheel, you need all six organizing principles working together in harmony to create a system that works. By creating sections and zones, finding the right storage solutions, corralling the information that comes at you all day long into an easy retrieval system, finding ways to take that information on the road, and of course, learning to get back to a comfortable starting place on a daily or weekly basis, you can stay organized in a way that supports who you are and how you live. To be organized is to be successful, and you, too, can have a beautiful and organized life.

"With organization comes empowerment."
—LYNDA PETERSON

SOMETIMES, EVEN AN ORGANIZER NEEDS HELP!

A couple of years ago, I moved into a brand-new home.

I had all of my boxes carefully numbered and listed on inventory sheets, ready to unpack as soon as my built-in cabinets were finished. In the meantime, I left the unopened boxes downstairs in the walk-out basement. One morning, I awoke to the sound of water gushing. After searching all over the house, I finally opened the door to the basement and was horrified to see water gushing out of the ceiling, as ceiling tiles fell like pancakes down to the floor and landed in about six inches of water. All the unpacked boxes were getting completely soaked. I ran upstairs and asked one of the exterior painters who

had been working on the house to help. He jumped into action and turned off the water to the whole house, then enlisted a few buddies to grab all the cardboard boxes and move them to a dry area. As they worked, they tore open each wet box and piled the contents in a huge heap on the dry side of the basement floor.

I learned that the entire mess had been caused by a loose freezer tube that had slipped out and fallen on the floor during the night, where it pushed out a gallon of water per minute all night long until I woke up and heard it. I had to move out of the house for six months, and it took about a year to complete all the repairs. In the meantime, the giant pile of books, papers, art supplies, memorabilia, photo albums, tax records, journals, home décor, old files, and clothes sat in the middle of the basement floor. When I moved back in, I would walk by it every few days, but I was too overwhelmed to wrap my head around sorting it all out. Finally, I called in a colleague, Julie Brooks of Peaceful Place Organizers, for support, and together we tackled

Ceiling tiles filled with water.

Waterlogged ceiling tiles on the floor.

Painter vacuuming up the water and pulling up the flooring.

Box contents spread all over the basement.

Thin tube from behind the freezer.

A dryer on warped floorboards.

More chaos.

from your basement ceiling, your life will surely bring its own curveballs, daily stressors, and minor catastrophes. But if you keep the three primary and the three secondary principles of *The Art of Organizing* in mind, you'll maintain your new

the mountain of stuff. Within a few hours, we had set up some shelving in the back of the unfinished basement and had the whole pile sorted and labeled so I could go about the task of putting everything away neatly throughout the house, wherever it belonged.

As this story shows, even the best organizational system can be strained by unexpected challenges. While I hope you'll never experience water gushing

Kitchen before renovation.

systems even in the face of major bumps in the road, like a move, career change, or basement flood. The same skills you used to get organized in the first place can help keep you on track no matter what life throws your way.

Basement cleaned up.

Before.

After: new floors and new paint jo.

INDEX

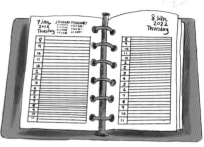

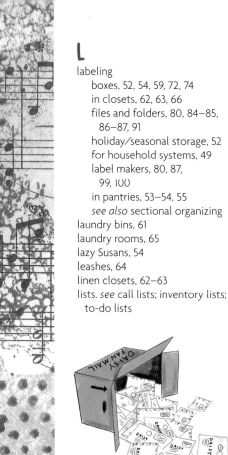
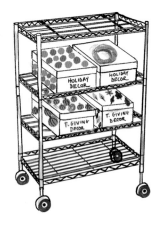

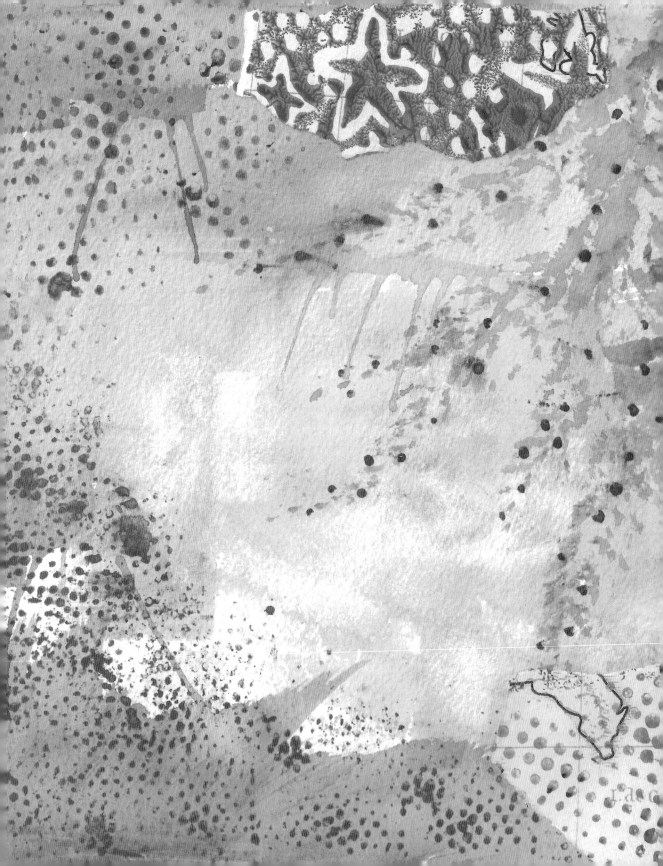

ACKNOWLEDGMENTS

I am deeply grateful to so many people who have helped me make this book come to life.

I am eternally grateful to Lindsay Ahl for your support and enthusiasm and helping me keep going. I couldn't have done this without you. I would also like to thank Jamie Cat Callan for encouraging my writing all those years ago. I would also like to express my deepest appreciation for Christine Lemay of Morningstar Design, who has been by my side every step of the way, bridging the gap between my ideas and bringing them to life on my website and all things technical. I would like to offer my deepest heartfelt appreciation to LeAnna Weller Smith of Weller Smith Design for helping me tremendously and guiding me every step of the way to create this beautiful book. You inspired me to bring this book to a whole new level. Thank you to your whole team of creative professionals for their talent and hard work.

To my editor, Christine McKnight, thank you for your incredible talent and for helping me artfully weave together the narrative for this book. My deepest appreciation goes to Farida Zaman for your tireless work and great talent to digitize all my illustrations.

A big thank you to Ann Treistman for introducing me to LeAnna. What a gift. I would also like to express my gratitude to Shannon Egan for copyediting and Samantha Holtgrewe for proofreading and indexing, and to Erin Williams for helping us get this across the finish line.

My deepest appreciation goes to my friends and family for their undying support and incredible generosity while I spent the time I needed to finish this book. To Suzie Baer, my soul sister, for being the most amazing friend I could ever ask for. To Nancy Cromer-Grayson for always believing in me, guiding me and for all your love. A very special thanks to Kim DeSisto for always being there for me as a wonderful friend and confidante, for making me feel like a part of the family and for opening your home to me; Karen Contreras for all the laughter even when I feel like crying; Deborah Winokur for making me feel like part of the family and for opening your heart and your home to me; and for Ian Rand, who introduced me to New York and helped plant the seed that led me on a path to realize all my creative dreams. A special thank you to Janet for always being there and for being my rock for so many years.

I would also like to express a special thanks to my cousin Lucy Geller for always inspiring me, and to my aunt, Tia Arlette, whose creativity and fearless creative expression taught me to think big and dream bigger. I would also like to thank Carol Pelletier Radford for so much inspiration, both spiritual and creative. Thank you for being a wonderful big sister! This has been a labor of love every step of the way. To anyone whose name I didn't mention, please know your help & support has been invaluable.

Testimonials

The Art of Organizing is a delightful and charming guide to organizing that is also practical and efficient. Nicole makes it easy to visualize your end result and stay inspired through the process of transforming your home and lifestyle. Her techniques are easy to remember and fun to apply. I have incorporated "Back-to-One" in my life, along with several other ideas, and it has changed my life! I highly recommend *The Art of Organizing*. —Lindsay A., Santa Fe, NM

The Art of Organizing is a simple, easy to follow approach for how to get organized. It is not a trendy collection of buzz words, but rather a step-by-step guide with a variety of real life examples. I can't wait to start organizing my own apartment!
—Deborah W., New York, NY

The Art of Organizing has given me motivation to organize my home in a way that makes sense for me! I can't wait to declutter my home (and brain) using your book as a road map to create better systems. —Karen C., New York, NY

I love this book! *The Art of Organizing* has so many great ideas to organize my life and I have already started to implement them. The illustrations help make this unique book easy to follow and memorable! —Kim D., Cape Cod, MA

Professional organizer Nicole Gabai has a unique talent of transforming a cluttered space into a well-designed, functional sanctuary. In *The Art of Organizing* she uses her 6 principles of organizing to explain how to create a home that is both practical and beautiful. She helps you assess each room, declutter it, and create a system that works so you may live an organized, stress-free life. —Susan B., Miami, FL

ABOUT THE AUTHOR

Nicole Gabai had an interest in organization long before she started her studies at Parsons School of Design and graduated from the Fashion Institute of Technology. Her childhood was filled with travel and adventure, living in Peru, France and the United States by the time she was seven. Organization became the way to calm the whirlwind life around her.

She has spent time working at MTV, and has been an actress and model in New York, Miami and Boston. She has taught workshops on organizing for companies such as Mercedes Benz, Bridgewater State College, Smith Barney, Susan B. Komen Foundation, and the Nantucket Chamber of Commerce. Nicole is also an artist and textile designer.

Nicole is a Golden Circle member of NAPO—the National Association of Productivity & Organizing Professionals—and a past historian of its South Florida chapter. Nicole travels to wherever her clients are but also offers a virtual platform to help people achieve their organizing goals.

Nicole lives on Cape Cod, where she organizes her fur-baby Luna's wardrobe and accessories closet and keeps her seashells in a lazy Susan with various compartments. Nicole is also a designer for homes and offices, helping people bridge the gap between beautiful and functional to maximize organizing capacity.

To order copies of the book, visit www.b-organized.net.
Follow her on Instagram @nicolegabai.

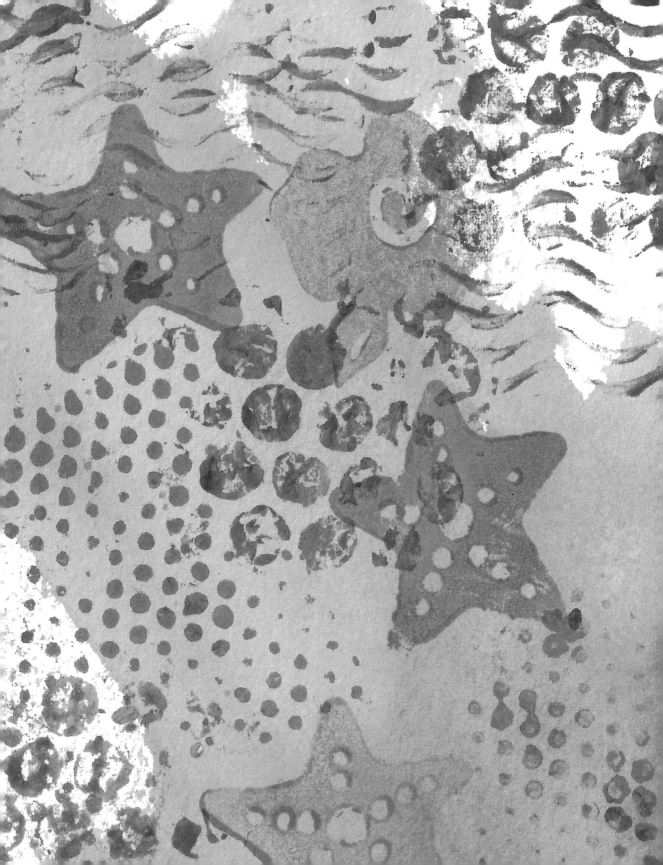